R. S. SURTEES

Mr. Sponge completely scatters his Lordship

R. S. SURTEES

BY

LEONARD COOPER

London

ARTHUR BARKER LTD.

First published in 1952

TO

ROSEMARY, LEO AND JOHN

Three werry certain comforts.

MADE AND PRINTED IN GREAT BRITAIN BY
MORRISON AND GIBB LIMITED, LONDON AND EDINBURGH

AUTHOR'S PREFACE

MANY Yorkshire authors have gratefully acknowledged their debt to Mr. Frank Beckwith, M.A., librarian of the Leeds Library, but few can have had better reason than I, since without his generous help and that of his staff I could hardly have written this book. I offer my sincere thanks to all of them—to Miss Cairns, Miss Jeff, Mr. Bumby and Mr. Walker for their tireless courtesy and ready response to my insatiable demands ; and to Mr. Beckwith himself for much help, more encouragement and yet more kindness.

I am grateful to Professor Bonamy Dobrée, O.B.E., for the loan of his articles in *The Times Literary Supplement* and for permission to quote from them ; to the librarian of the Bradford City Library for the loan of books ; to Messrs. A. M. Heath & Co. Ltd., for their help and courtesy.

I must pay tribute to the memory of my father, who introduced me to Mr. Jorrocks and Soapey Sponge ; and above all to my sisters, Lettice and Barbara, at whose suggestion I began to write this book and whose help, criticism and encouragement have sustained me throughout its progress.

CONTENTS

LIST OF ILLUSTRATIONS

BLACK AND WHITE ILLUSTRATIONS

COLOUR ILLUSTRATIONS

CHAPTER I

The Puppy at Walk

" If you should adopt this method, you must remember to use them early to go in couples : and when they become of proper age they must be walked out often : for should they remain confined, they would neither have the shape, health, or understanding, which they ought to have."—PETER BECKFORD.

" I often think," continued Mr. Jorrocks musingly, " that it would be a capital thing to pass ingenuous youth generally through a sort of Chobham camp to learn 'em wot they can really do without."—*Handley Cross.*

I

" 'UNTIN'," said Mr. Jorrocks at the dinner of the Handley Cross Hounds, " is the foremost passion of my 'eart ! Compared with it all others are flat and unprofitable. It's not never of no manner of use 'umbuggin' about the matter, but there's no sport fit to hold a candle to fox-'untin'."

To such a belief Robert Smith Surtees was born in 1805, the year of Trafalgar, and in such a tradition he was brought up. His grandfather had kept foxhounds, his father kept both foxhounds and harriers. Later on in life for a short time he was to keep his own pack. Hunting was in his blood and in his family, who were scattered over the County of Durham, at Hamsterley, Redworth, Dinsdale and Mainsforth.

The branch to which he himself belonged lived at Milkwell Burn, near Newcastle, from the time of Charles II till 1810, when they bought Hamsterley Hall from the Swinburne family. The earliest date from which the stock can be traced is about the beginning of the eleventh century.

The authority for this statement is the elder Robert Surtees of Mainsforth, cousin of the novelist, antiquary and the author of that monumental work *The History of the County of Durham.* Surtees of Mainsforth, the only other author in the family, deserves more than a passing mention, if only for the reason that, alone among the Surtees clan, he hated hunting. The two Roberts were the literary members of the family, and they shared the satiric humour which led in one case to the Border Ballads and in the other to Soapey Sponge and Facey Romford. Both of them went at one time to London to read law, and both returned to family properties in County Durham. They shared that devotion to the land and to their county which drove the elder to study and record its antiquities, and the younger to follow and improve its agriculture. No doubt they met, though there is no record of their having done so, but it can hardly be likely that they found each other congenial.

Fortunately Anthony Surtees, the novelist's father, was thoroughly congenial—" a thorough paced sportsman," his son calls him. Robert Surtees tells a typical story of his schooldays when, wandering about the stable yard, he heard a pack of hounds in a neighbouring wood and rushing to the stables pulled out the nearest horse and rode it, clothing and all, in the direction of the hounds. There, somewhat to his alarm —for he was not supposed to be out—he met his father, also mounted, who seemed to think it rather a good joke to see a horse out hunting in clothing and without a saddle, and merely said, " But damn it, lad, why did not you take the sheets off ? "

Another genial picture of Anthony Surtees comes from " Nimrod," Charles James Apperley, the hunting correspondent who was later so to anger Robert Surtees as to drive him to his bitterest satire in the " Pomponius Ego " episode in *Handley Cross*. Apperley was on a tour of the Yorkshire packs and was " commanded—not invited," to Hamsterley (where for the first time he met Mr. Surtees, jun., his future enemy).

" The Squire of Hamsterley," Nimrod wrote in his characteristically high-flown style, " is not to my knowledge an author, but ' every inch of him ' a sportsman : yet who more proper than himself to write on the antiquities of any County ?—he being a most religious observer of the remains of ancient times, in the unbounded hospitality of his house and table ; one who it might be imagined had himself existed in those ancient times when men had high notions of the rights of hospitality, and not merely the rules of civility and when, as Homer says, strangers were received as guests from heaven—one who thinks with me that the over-refinements of polished life are but a mask for insincerity and heartlessness and in short a true sample of the old English Squire, and as good a judge of a horse, a hound, a bottle of port-wine and an oak-tree, as any man in England or anywhere else." And he ends with the heartfelt comment, " I drank more claret during the five or six days

I spent at Hamsterley than I had done in that space of time for many a long day before."

Of Robert Surtees Nimrod records that " Mr. Surtees jun. accompanied the carriage " and Surtees himself has left an account of the meeting. This was in 1834, when Robert Surtees was twenty-nine and only just before the beginning of that desultory and unworthy squabble which only ended with Nimrod's death in 1843. It was four years before Anthony Surtees died and his son succeeded to Hamsterley Hall.

The records of Robert Smith Surtees' childhood are pitifully few. He was no diarist, though he kept from to time to time a record of his doings on odd scraps of paper, many of which were defaced or lost.

He was born on 17th May 1805 at The Riding, Northumberland, and baptized on 21st August 1806 at Bywell St. Andrew. His own account of his life begins with his entry to Ovingham School, but he does not mention the date. It must have been some years before 1818, the first date accurately recorded since his baptism and the year when he went to Durham Grammar School.

All we know of him in the meantime is the fact that he hunted with his father's hounds and also with the more famous pack of Mr. Ralph Lambton. In both he was fortunate. Anthony Surtees' hounds were a small private pack, the field were mostly farmers. The country was difficult and hilly, adapted rather for slow methodical hunting than for the fast gallops of the Midlands. In such a country a boy could learn to hunt rather than ride to hounds, to watch hounds work rather than to cut across country. He could learn the craft from the beginning and come to appreciate the wealth of unseen detail that makes up so much of the huntsman's job. That he did learn his lesson thoroughly is evident in all his novels, and his attitude towards horses and hounds is eloquent of it. But Anthony Surtees was also a " master of muggers," and his son is always kind to the sport. " Nor was Surtees a snob even in hunting," says Professor Bonamy Dobrée, " in the way that Nimrod was : he despised the carted stag variety, it is true, for ' when you've catched the stag, you're no better off than ye were before,' as Jimmy observed to Mr. Romford : but he was friends with the currant-jelly men : the excellent Major Yammerton is not held up to ridicule, and one of the best descriptions of a hunt is that of the hare with the Goose and Dumpling Folk in *Hawbuck Grange*." Moreover, he even goes so far on one or two occasions as to show an almost shamefaced sympathy with the hunted hare.

He was learning other lessons at the same time, because it was his good fortune to hunt in his early years with Mr. Ralph Lambton's hounds, whose country adjoined that hunted by his father. There could have been no better teacher or finer example of an M.F.H. than Ralph Lambton, Member of Parliament for Durham City, and for over forty years a master of hounds. He was a man of more education than most of the neighbouring squires, of complete integrity, high principles and personal austerity. His portrait, by Sir Francis Grant, painted in his later years, shows a face of singular dignity.

Surtees' talent ran always to observation rather than to imagination. His works are peopled with the men whom he met in real life, often more thinly disguised than is usual with most authors. Even before he went to Durham Grammar School at the age of thirteen, he had observed and tucked away for future reference his private schoolmaster. Such a master of hounds as Ralph Lambton must have produced a deep impression on him in those early days, and it is evident that throughout his life Surtees remembered him and kept him before his eyes as his ideal M.F.H. Indeed it is probably to Lambton that he owes his conviction of the essential dignity and importance of that office.

II

It is a pity that we know so little of those early days at Hamsterley and that the little that we do know is concerned with sport. That the young Robert's relations with his father were friendly we know, but of those with his mother we have no trace. His elder brother, Anthony, died in 1831, when Robert was sixteen, leaving him heir to Hamsterley; and six years later his mother died, to be outlived by only one year by her husband. So Robert succeeded to Hamsterley in 1838, and the records thereafter, though scanty enough, are a little fuller. But we would gladly know what the earlier life at Hamsterley was like in those formative years between 1805, when he was born, and the uncertain date when he went to Ovingham School and his own diary, such as it is, begins.

The impression remains of a typical country house of the period, where food and drink were plentiful and the main pre-occupation was with sport. There is an overwhelming impression, too, of an exclusively male atmosphere, which is borne out in Surtees' later work. Surely there has never been a novelist of the same importance who knew and cared so little about women.

To Mr. Jorrocks women are " werry weary warmints." To Facey Romford they are a nuisance in the hunting field, because "they are always getting in the way." In all the Surtees novels there are only two or three women who remain in the memory—chiefly, Angelena Blunt, Mrs. Jorrocks and Lucy Glitters, and (for their names only) those inimitable domestic servants Dirty No. 1, Dirty No. 2, Dirty No. 3 and Dirtiest of the Dirty.

It is easy to receive the impression that this lack of interest and knowledge was the result of the exclusively male atmosphere of sport and the absence of feminine influence that surrounded his early formative years.

It would be interesting, too, to know more of the domestic economy of Hamsterley if only because of the curious hatred for domestic servants which is evident throughout the novels. Butlers are usually drunken and dishonest, maid-servants always slatternly and dirty, grooms and stablemen almost always insolent and idle. Country squires are, or were, usually well served by the sons and daughters of their tenants, and it seems unlikely that Anthony Surtees would have tolerated anyone about his stables or kennels who was neither competent nor civil. Robert Surtees was later to travel into most of the English hunting counties and to know the pleasures and miseries of a guest at country houses and inns. It may well be that it was during this time, which he spent as a hunting correspondent, that he acquired his dislike for servants. Yet it is persistent and evident in a way that suggests a derivation from impressionable youth. Perhaps the seed was implanted in youth and flowered in the later years together with those two other aversions of his which form the target for so much of his satire. And these two, hatred of the regular army and contempt for the aristocracy, can hardly have been implanted in those earliest years.

The Hamsterley packs were a small private concern, and it is unlikely that many cavalry officers took the trouble to come far across difficult country to hunt with them. He may have encountered a few with Lambton's hounds, but even that is unlikely. These aversions, which really form the basis of Surtees' later satirical novels, will appear in greater detail when the time comes to assess him as a novelist and a satirist. But they must be briefly set down here, because in some degree they spring from that other background of his youth, that life at Hamsterley of which we know all too little either from himself or from any other source. All his life the most important thing to him was hunting—and hunting as he had known it with the Hamsterley and Lambton packs. That was his norm, his standard of comparison, and any deviation from it was to him either ridiculous or vicious. It accounts for his dislike of Nimrod and his flamboyant accounts of fast gallops, for his jeers at cockney hunts and Boulogne hounds, for his contempt for the "show-packs" of the aristocracy. It accounts, too, for his sympathy with, and understanding of, such packs as The Goose and Dumpling and the Flat Hat, and Mr. Jovey Jessop's and Major Yammerton's hounds, because they hunted the fox or the hare with the same earnestness as they used to hunt them at Hamsterley. Hamsterley was his background for nearly all his life. He died in 1865 at the age of sixty and for only eighteen of those years was he absent from his home. It was a typical nineteenth-century country squire's home, a background of hounds and horses, port and claret, game and beef-steaks, country sport and country duties. And, apart from what he called "a taste for scribbling," he was a typical product of it—honest, conscientious, opinionated, resentful and suspicious of anything that did not conform to his somewhat rigid standards. He knew and fulfilled the duties as well as he enjoyed the sport and privileges of a country squire. His upbringing had taught him his responsibility to the land and to the people who worked on it.

Hamsterley and the hunting field are his real setting, as they were his first and most important education in the first ten or twelve years of his life. But his formal education was soon to begin, though unfortunately the actual date of it is lost. It must have been some time about the date of Waterloo when he was sent away to his first school at Ovingham.

III

There is a depressing similarity about the reminiscences of schoolboys of the eighteenth and early nineteenth centuries. The methods and aims of public and private schools had hardly varied since such schools came into being. And they were not to vary seriously till Arnold of Rugby revolutionized them with his startling innovations of compulsory games and the prefectorial system, and, years later, Sewell of Radley realized the necessity of the arts in any system of education.

But in the early years of the nineteenth century the curriculum at nearly all such schools had a delightful simplicity—the classics before everything, a lot of scripture and a little mathematics, a liberal use of the birch and anything but a liberal supply of food. Boys, it was thought, were like young wild animals, best controlled and kept out of mischief by whipping and underfeeding. Masters, it was realized, must live and make enough money to retire on, and the less they gave their pupils to eat the more profit they could make. It seems a far cry from Eton to Dotheboys Hall, but there is a similarity in their methods. No doubt the Etonians of that day did not weed their tutors' gardens nor clean their houses, but there was little difference between the disciplinary methods of Dr. Keate (who once flogged his whole confirmation class under the impression that they were the day's defaulters) and Mr. Wackford Squeers.

The school to which Robert Surtees was sent was at Ovingham, about seven miles from Hamsterley, and was kept by the Rev. James Birkett. It was a private school of some standing, for Surtees says himself that, "Here formerly many of the aristocracy of the North received the rudiments of their education. Many of the Loraines, all the Blacketts of Wylam were there; the Allgoods of Nunwick were there; Robert Ingham, M.P. for South Shields, was there; John Hodgson Hinde, who so ably represented Newcastle-on-Tyne for so many years in Parliament, was there; his brother Richard Hodgson, long M.P. for Berwick, now for Tynemouth, was there."

The Rev. James Birkett was no doubt indistinguishable from hundreds of other private-school masters of the period. "He combined the business of schoolmaster with that of a gardener, farmer and walking-stick maker." That last occupation of his earned him something more than local or temporary fame. He stands out as the first of those real people whom Surtees knew and observed, and whom he later used as the basis for the comic characters of his novels.

"He had," Surtees writes, "the most ludicrous propensity for making and hoarding up walking-sticks that ever was heard of. He could not see or hear of a promising sapling but that he would be at it and, having converted it into a walking-stick, would add it to his already redundant collection. Every garret and spare place about the house was full of them: they must have been counted by thousands, and he wouldn't give one away if it was ever so. I firmly believe that he thought he was amassing a fortune for his successors therewith." Forty years later *Mr. Sponge's Sporting Tour* was published. In it is Mr. Jogglebury Crowdey, sneaking out at night to steal his neighbour's saplings, carving them into "gibbey-sticks" and laying them away in an attic as an investment for his descendants. "In the farming line," Surtees continues, "Birkett had a famous breed of horses that he was always talking of selling to the King, but I don't know that he ever accomplished his object. The South country dealers used to come and look at them and drink his rum and milk—a beverage of which he was particularly fond —but I think in all probability he would be too high-minded in his price when it came to the point."

There was no particular reason why Birkett should have been high-minded in his price. His labour cost him little enough. Surtees makes no complaint of the discipline at Ovingham and he chronicles the domestic arrangements with a humorous detachment. He devotes more space in his papers to the few years which he spent at Ovingham than to the whole of his childhood at Hamsterley. But most men love to reminisce about their schooldays, and Surtees is no exception.

"It was a primitive establishment and for the benefit of posterity I will describe the arrangements. There were two good-sized bedrooms, each holding about eight beds, into which the boys were divided without much discrimination. The beds had white counterpanes, which, however, only appeared on high days when company were coming, those in ordinary wear being of the more serviceable colours of drab and green—drab on one side and green on the other. That, however, I believe is an arrangement not altogether peculiar to my day.

"Well then, we used to rise at seven or eight o'clock in the morning, according to the season of the year, and proceed to a little washing-room adjoining and common to both apartments, in which were four basins and four roller towels against the wall. There were no jugs and no convenience for changing the water, so the last comer had it anything but pure. The insoluble soap was like a square of ivory, it was so hard and slippery. The ablutions, such as they were, had to be performed with one's hands—sponges, tooth-brushes, nail-brushes, anything of that sort being considered superfluous. Such a thing as a looking-glass was altogether unthought of: each boy had to take his appearance on credit."

Lack of washing facilities is not one which arouses a passion of resentment in the breasts of most small boys, but breakfast is a more serious matter.

"Dressed and downstairs the ceremony of breakfast commences. Not that there was much ceremony, for it was quite in the rough—no table cloth, no knives, no forks, no cups and saucers, no nothing in the crockery way. A large bread basket full of knotches and hunches of brown bread, together with a tin pot full of milk for each boy, having been duly deposited on a dresser, the school formed in single file and marched past, each boy appropriating as much bread as he thought he could consume and a can of milk. With these they returned to their places at the desks in the schoolroom. Supper was an exact repetition of breakfast, save that occasionally, as a great treat, we had beer and leathery cheese or roast potatoes and dripping, fare at which servants of the present day would turn up their noses, and think themselves dreadfully ill-used if it were offered to them.

"Dinner was a more sumptuous meal, being served in the master's parlour, where there was a cloth to the table and a carpet to the flagged floor. Grace being said, pudding came before meat, and generally consisted of a long slimey roll pudding made of the aforesaid gooseberries, but wherein jam played a very subordinate part to the paste, or apple dumplings—the apples the produce of the orchard—or spice puddings as they were called, wherein the currants were few and far between—one or other of these delicacies being duly discussed before the meat, which was generally a round of home-fed beef, over whose merits old Birkett used to deliver an exordium as he stood and carved it. Beer was the beverage."

They were not badly off considering the times in which they lived and the total ignorance in both schools and homes of the elementary principles of diet. It seems appalling to a generation, one of whose great public schools includes oranges and grapefruit in the dietary and issues vitamin pills to the young gentlemen (who carefully conserve them and shoot them out of their rifles on J.T.C. field-days). But at Ovingham there was fresh fruit from the gardens, a luxury practically unheard of in schools of that day, home-fed beef and milk from the farm. And if there was nothing but bread for breakfast, at least each boy could take as much as he thought he could consume, which was not the case at Dotheboys Hall.

There is little more to be said of Ovingham. The Rev. James Birkett survives in the Jogglebury Crowdey of *Mr. Sponge's Sporting Tour* and probably in the description in *Hillingdon Hall* of the schoolmaster, Mr. Slooman.

"Slooman being on the best of terms with himself, coughed and hemmed and stroked his chin, and looked compacently around, as much as to say, 'I am Sir Oracle, and when I ope my lips let no dog bark.' He was a little, bristly-headed, badger-eyed, pedantic, radical schoolmaster, who farmed his own glebe, and managed matters somewhat in the style of the celebrated Wackford Squeers, frequently recreating the boys with a little work on the farm."

Surtees left Ovingham in 1818 and went to Durham Grammar School, where he stayed for only one year. He left no record of any sort of his life there, nor have his biographers been able to discover anything about it. It would be intensely interesting, in view of his later career, to know what he learned in the academic sense both at Ovingham and Durham—if indeed he learned anything at all. Presumably his education was mainly classical, because such was the education in all public schools at the time.

IV

The irritating uncertainty about dates pursues us yet for a few years and we have no record at all of the years 1819 to 1822. That Surtees left Durham School in 1819 is certain; and according to the Law Society's records, he was articled to Mr. Purvis on 22nd of April 1822. Mr. E. D. Cuming, who in 1924 edited Surtees' private papers, took some trouble to test a theory that he spent those three years at a university. But he says, " The lists of graduates at Oxford and Cambridge do not include his name, and he was not at Durham University." But in any case in 1819 Surtees was only fourteen, and though men went younger to the university in those days than they do now, it is almost inconceivable that any university would have admitted a boy of that age. (But Mr. Cuming assumes the year 1803 as the date of birth.)

Mr. Frederick Watson, writing in 1933, conjectures much more reasonably that he went to work for Mr. Purvis soon after leaving school but was not articled until 1822, the date given by the Law Society's records, which seem incontrovertible. All we can say for certain is that he was articled to Mr. Purvis in that year and that he remained with him for three years. Five years is the full term for an articled pupil and, again according to the Law Society's records, he was " further articled " on 17th May 1825 to Mr. William Bell of Bow Churchyard in London.

The choice of a legal career for Robert Surtees was almost inevitable, for in those days only three professions, the Services, the Church and the Law were possible for the sons of county families.

There was no naval or military tradition in the Surtees family, and indeed, if his later feelings about the army had their origin in his early life, there was even a strong feeling against it. Nor was there any of that taste for scholarship which, combined with the reversion of a good family living, so often attracted younger sons to the Church. But the Law, besides being a suitable occupation for a gentleman, might later be useful to a man who would inherit an estate, sit on the county bench and find himself in situations where a knowledge of conveyancing, the game laws and the law of trespass might be of value. Robert was a younger son, but his elder brother, Anthony, died in 1831 and Robert became the heir to Hamsterley. To speak of the Law as a career for him is probably incorrect. It was at the most a gentlemanly way of passing the time and acquiring useful knowledge until he should return either to Hamsterley or to some other estate, there to hunt, to administer justice and live the life of his forbears.

He does not seem to have regarded it himself in the light of a career nor to have taken any interest in it. While he was at Newcastle, more or less under the parental eye, he probably had to give some attention to his duties in the office. But when he moved to London his memories, which at this period of his life are much fuller, make little or no mention of his studies. Life in London, hunting at Brighton and Boulogne proved an irresistible counter-attraction. Finally his "taste for scribbling" took precedence of everything except hunting, and, after being admitted in Chancery in 1828, he abandoned the Law altogether and began to write for the *Sporting Magazine* till 1831, when he was installed by the publisher Ackermann as editor of the *New Sporting Magazine*.

The life of a law student was not an enviable one, if the experience of Charley Stobbs in *Handley Cross* when he was articled to Mr. Twister of Lincoln's Inn Square is anything like the reality.

"Mr. Twister was one of those legal nuisances called conveyancers, whom it is to be hoped some contrivance will be found to extinguish, and he could find a loop-hole for an unwilling purchaser to creep out of in the very best of titles. Having plenty to do himself, he took as many pupils as ever he could get, to help each other to do nothing. Each of these paid him a hundred guineas a year, in return for which they had the run of a dingy, carpetless room, the use of some repulsive-looking desks, and liberty to copy twenty volumes of manuscript precedents, that the great Mr. Twister had copied himself when a pupil with great Mr. Somebody-else." The staff at Mr. Twister's when Charley Stobbs arrived consisted of Mr. Bill Bowker the managing clerk, Mr. Frost and Mr. Jones, two articled pupils, "working men with their ways to make in the world, they had paid their hundred guineas for a high-sounding name and betaken themselves to the mechanical drudgery of precedent copying, with an industry worthy of a better direction"; and the Hon. Henry Lollington, the ninth son of an Earl.

The Law was then an overcrowded profession, especially in its lower ranks, and the pupils at Mr. Twister's are typical of the entrants to that profession. There were the "saps" or "working men," and there were the gentlemen, like Surtees himself, idling away the days until they could escape into the freedom of a country estate or into journalism and literature. And how many of them did escape into literature we realize when it is remembered that the list of articled pupils and lawyer's clerks in the nineteenth century included Thackeray, Dickens, Surtees, Harrison Ainsworth, Macaulay, Charles Reade, Kinglake and Blackmore.

When in 1825 he left Newcastle to be "further articled" to Mr. William Bell, of Bow Churchyard, London, he travelled by coach, for railways were still in their infancy. Surtees mentions in his schooldays' reminiscences that "the first locomotive engine was to be seen in my early days, puffing and blowing and straining itself on the Wylam Colliery waggon-way down to the village of Newburn. I perfectly remember its black ugly features and discordant noises. The thing was considered a great nuisance and many were the devices set afoot to put it down."

Most of the devices were set on foot by the Duke of Northumberland, whose Castle of Alnwick was a few miles away from the waggon-way. The engine in question had been constructed by William Hedley in 1813 to replace horse-draught at Wylam Colliery. The Duke, though his castle was out of sight and sound of the waggon-way, took violent exception to the engine, the more so that its owner had certain way-leaves over the Alnwick estate. He consulted his man of law, who found himself in the difficult position of having to please His Grace and at the same time to make the best of a thoroughly bad case. Extracts from his Opinion are quoted by Mr. E. D. Cuming and show how the unhappy man of law tried to extricate himself from his predicament. "He was bound to admit that it did not appear to him that any objection could be taken to this offensive novelty on the terms of the wayleaves lease or agreement itself": adding, "but I think the use of such an engine

Mr. Jorrocks at Ongar Castle

[HANDLEY CROSS]

may be deemed a nuisance to A. [the Duke] if the smoke and noise so occasioned and the distance of the house of A. render his habitation unhealthy or uncomfortable. But this must depend entirely upon the quantity of smoke and noise so occasioned, and the distance of the house of A. from the waggon-way."

As the house of A. was at such a distance from the waggon-way that its owner could neither see, smell nor hear the engine, it was difficult to show that it had been rendered either unhealthy or uncomfortable. So the man of law fell back on his second line of defence. "If the engine disturbs the cattle grazing on the lands adjacent to the waggon-way so as to injure them with regard to their feeding, I think it may be regarded as a nuisance."

"Apparently," says Mr. Cuming, "it could not be shown that the cattle did suffer from the inconvenience, and the Duke was obliged to let the matter rest."

But the forces of reaction were not yet defeated. A month later a neighbouring land-owner, whose house was actually within two-thirds of a mile of the waggon-way, joined in the attack and laid his case before a Mr. Losh, barrister-at-law, and brother of the County Court judge of Northumberland. But he was no more fortunate, for Mr. Losh advised that the injury done was scarcely sufficient to justify an action for damages, and that "unless some actual injury to the health or personal security of the neighbours or passengers can be proved, I do not think an indictment for a public nuisance would be successful."

Surtees' attitude towards railways was the same as the Duke's and as that of most big land-owners of their day. To-day in country districts there are hundreds of villages over a mile away from their stations because of the stout resistance of the local squire to the encroaching engine. With Surtees as with all of them it was a simple and consistent attitude compounded of a countryman's suspicion of anything urban, a horseman's of anything mechanical, and a Tory's of anything new.

"Passing through Darlington," Surtees wrote, "I saw several coaches that travel on the rail-roads. They are drawn by one horse, the resistance being trifling: these coaches have a box at each end for reasons that were obvious, and their dirty appearance seemed well adapted to the passengers who travel in them." If the horse-drawn rail-roads were dirty, the new locomotive roads must have been filthy beyond belief. But it was in the spring of 1825 when Surtees set off for London—and he travelled, as a gentleman should, by coach.

"I travelled," he says, "up from Newcastle-on-Tyne by the old Highflyer coach, to catch which at eight o'clock in the morning I had to leave Hamsterley between five and six. Then by a steady persevering grind continued all through that day, all that night and all the following day, we reached the dismal White Horse in Fetter Lane at eight that night. The fare was £6 inside and it was considered very fine travelling."

So for two days and one night he passed over the changing face of England—from the moors of his own county, through the stone-walled hills and broad pastures of Yorkshire, through the flat fen-land of Lincoln and through the green fields and big hedges of Leicestershire—Mr. Jorrocks's "cut 'em down and 'ang 'em out to dry" country. He must have passed through and observed, with what interest we can imagine, the countries of a dozen of those famous packs whose names sound in the ears of hunting men like a solemn litany—the Marquis of Zetland's, the York and Ainsty, the Bramham Moor, the Badsworth; Lord Fitzwilliam's, the Quorn, the Belvoir, the Pytchley, the Woodland Pytchley, the Cottesmore—some already of long standing, some in their infancy, some yet unheard of, some still hunting the wild stag. It was the old England, that he understood and knew, the England of Hamsterley and Mr. Lambton's hounds. But he must have seen, too, unmistakable signs of the new England that he was never really to know or understand—the smoking chimneys of Yorkshire woollen-mills where the weavers and spinners were going to work instead of doing their allotted task at home: gaunt pit-heads rising in the north Midlands; estates beginning to show the effect of the lack of that labour that was already beginning to drift to the town. For, though the young Surtees could not know it, England was changing; and the change was to bring down his class and his like, to set up money as the standard instead of land or breeding, to put the town before the country, industry before agriculture, and success before everything, as surely as the railways were replacing coaches like the Highflyer, which rolled so gaily out of Biggleswade, driven by "a steady old gentleman called Bates, who drove his own horses and was uncommonly careful of them." New ideas travel slowly over the north-country moors, and hunting squires are notoriously slow to accept them. Hardly a breath of the new wind of democracy and industry that was sweeping across England can have reached Hamsterley. It is important to realize this, because the ideas and convictions that had already been formed in the young Surtees were to stay with him all his life. It had been a sheltered life so far—home and school, hunting and country. He had not even had the chance of encountering new ideas and different types that a public school and university might have given him. In the Newcastle office he was still under his family's influences, his life still centred on Hamsterley and the fox-hounds and horses. Even his school friends came from the same kind of home, Blackett of Wylam, Allgood of Nunwick, Ingham, Hindle and Hodgson. He started on this journey to London knowing, surely, as little of the world as any young hero of a fairy-tale setting off to make his fortune.

There was then a pleasing custom of decorating the horses' heads with flowers for the last stage of their journey. " The coach entered London by the long continuous town of Tottenham, and the last change of horses, I remember, had their heads decorated with holly-hocks: they were a capital team and in beautiful condition. It was an imposing entry into London; for after the villa and semi-detached villa scenery of the suburbs, with innumerable gigs and one-horse vehicles, the coach took its way right through the heart of the city, past the Exchange, the Bank of England, The Mansion House and St. Paul's, so on down Snow Hill, up Holborn Hill to the aforesaid White Horse in Fetter Lane."

CHAPTER II

The Young Entry

" It is now time to stoop them to a scent. You had better enter them at their own game : it will save you much trouble afterwards."—PETER BECKFORD.

" Ingenuous youth 'aving now got all the implements 'o the chase scraped together, and the early rains of dear delightful November—the best and plisantest month i' the year—'aving well salivated the ground, forthwith let 'im put my precepts in practice."—*Handley Cross*.

I

IF the face of England was changing, the face of London, in the West End at any rate, was already changed ; and the change was still going on. George, Prince of Wales, Prince Regent and King, had many faults, but he had one transcendent merit. He could recognize genius, and he was always ready to back it to the limit of his resources and beyond them. In John Nash he found the genius whom he needed for his grandiose scheme of transforming London and outrunning the Emperor Napoleon's rebuilding of Paris.

By the spring of 1825 the greater part of the work was done. The Regent's Park and Canal, Regent Street itself, with the quadrant and the lovely curve, were already in being. The clearing of the future Trafalgar Square had been begun and plans had been drawn for the new National Gallery on its northern side. Carlton House, the Prince Regent's headquarters for so many years, was marked for destruction and Buckingham House was about to be altered to make a king's palace. Carlton House Terrace was designed and work would start on it as soon as Carlton House itself should be demolished. " I really think," said Crabb Robinson, after driving round the new sites in a gig, " this enclosure with the new Street leading to it from Carlton House, will give a sort of glory to the Regent's Government, which will be more felt by remote posterity than the victories of Trafalgar and Waterloo, glorious as these are."

Oxford Street was still the northern boundary of fashionable London, so much so that Nash, in his original plan, suggested the creation of

Oxford Circus, "to remove the impression that the street had been crossed." But already squares and houses were beginning to rise north of the street and in the direction of St. John's Wood and Mr. William Lord's cricket ground. The Zoological Gardens were opened in 1828, and the citizens of London and their children found feeding the bears there a pleasant change from feeding the lions at the Tower. But the tide of fashion moves slowly and Hyde Park was still its main channel.

"London," Surtees wrote later in his memoirs, "though perhaps scarcely more than half the size it is now was more imposing, more concentrated. You had all the great people there without the little ones. Hyde Park was a magnificent sight, especially on a Sunday. The fashionable drive was between . . . and Cumberland Gate, though the greater crush was between . . . and Grosvenor Gate (the manuscript is defaced and the other names are lost).

"There was more walking—promenading, rather—in Kensington Gardens than in Hyde Park. The magnates of the land having shown their equipages would afterwards show themselves in the Gardens, where on a fine Sunday the beauty and brilliance of the scene could not be surpassed. The spreading boughs of tall elms on either side of the South Walk, almost meeting overhead, formed a perfect canopy, under which the rank and fashion used to promenade on the smooth turf. Soldiers and liveried servants were not admitted, nor indeed anyone whose appearance the gate-keepers did not consider respectable. None of the great unwashed were to be seen in the Park in those days."

It was a gay London for those who lived within the quadrilateral—if not for those thousands of the great unwashed who lived beyond it. George IV had been king for five years, but much of the old Regency splendour and jollity remained and the great figures of the last reign were to be seen in the streets. The Duke of Wellington mounted his horse at Apsley House and rode to Westminster, touching his hat to the crowd. The Marquess of Anglesea in white top-hat and blue frock-coat rode in Rotten Row. Long Wellesley, afterwards Earl of Mornington, was "enunciating the notable doctrine that no one could live like a gentleman in England on less than fifty thousand a year." Wilberforce was living at Gore House (the site of the present Albert Hall) later to be better known as the home of Lady Blessington. And Count D'Orsay "set up the handsomest ombrella in London and valked in Kensington Gardens on Sunday, the only day when he could be safe from the bailiffs." There was dancing at Almack's and gambling at Crockford's, though play never ran so high again as in the days of Charles James Fox. According to Mr. Francis Coghlan's book *The Cicerone or Fashionable Guide to all the Places of Public Amusement* there were a dozen theatres open in London in 1830. The Lyceum had been destroyed by fire in 1825, but there were Drury Lane, with its tradition of Garrick, Keane, Sheridan and the elder Kemble, where *The School for Scandal* and *The Rivals* were still regular pillars of the repertory and the box-office; Covent Garden where the younger Kemble, Charles, was playing Othello, Coriolanus and Benedict; the King's Theatre in the Haymarket; The Theatre Royal or English Opera House in the Strand; the Adelphi; the Savoy; Astley's Amphitheatre; the Cobourg; Sadler's Wells; the West London in Tottenham Street; the Olympic in the Strand; and the latest marvel, the Haymarket, rebuilt by Nash at a cost of £18,000 and opened in 1821.

The pleasure gardens were still popular, though with a less fashionable clientele than in the previous century. Vauxhall Gardens had another twenty years of life before them, Cremorne another fifty, though Ranelagh had closed in 1803. The entertainments there included fireworks, balloon ascents, orchestras and that rack-punch which Jos. Sedley found so insidious and so deadly. But if it was a gay London for those who could ride in Hyde Park and walk in Kensington Gardens it was anything but gay for the much larger proportion of its inhabitants who were not "respectable" enough to be admitted.

Surtees must have known something of the dreary life of chop-house and cigar-shop, for in one of his "Sportin' Lectors" Mr. Jorrocks describes in detail and with feeling the miseries of the countryman who comes up to London to see the sights—the man to whom Almack's and Crockford's are closed but who is too superior for the robust joys of the Cider-Cellar.

But these are the miseries of a man who, while not in the social swim, is still south of Oxford Street and west of the Strand. East of that line and south of the river, life was very different. There were poverty, drunkenness, disease, misery and crime. It was not long since the Prince Regent himself had been attacked and robbed within two miles of Carlton House. Highwaymen and footpads still haunted the roads out of London, and in the West End itself the streets were unsafe after dark. All the district round Soho and Covent Garden was a wilderness of cess-pits, burial-grounds and hovels. The men who lived in the dark underworld that underlay the splendour of Nash's new London were desperately poor, brutal, as frequently drunk as they could afford, when a man could get dead drunk for a few pence. And in 1825 all the old brutal blood-sports were alive in the East End of London, and that Surtees himself saw them is evident from the grim description in *Handley Cross.*

"From the centre of the unceiled, hugely rafted roof of a spacious building hung an iron hoop, stuck round with various lengths of tallow candles, lighting an oval pit, in which two savage bull-dogs were rolling and tearing each other about, under the auspices of their coatless masters, who stood at either end applauding their exertions. A vast concourse of ruffianly spectators occupied the benches, rising gradually from the pit towards the rafters, along which some were carelessly stretched, lost in ecstasy at the scene below."

That scene and others like it made a profound and lasting impression on the mind of the young Surtees. All his life he set his face against the evils of betting and against the more cruel blood-sports. To the non-sporting mind there is nothing particularly humane in chasing a fox or a hare until it is too weary to run any longer and letting it, at the end of its gasping agony, be torn to pieces by dogs. But Surtees with his upbringing could not be expected to feel this—though he does sometimes show pity for the hunted hare. He was rigidly opposed to the sports that he really considered cruel, and in 1832, when he started the *New Sporting Magazine*, he made his position perfectly clear. "We expressly stated in our prospectus," he writes, "that Prize-fighting, Bull-baiting and Cock-fighting were low and demoralizing pursuits and all reference thereto was to be excluded from our pages."

Horse-racing, too, he regarded with disfavour, mainly on account of his feeling against betting, though he was obliged to admit it to the columns of the *New Sporting Magazine*. But, for himself, though he went racing in London and Brighton, Paris and Boulogne, he never cared for it. For one thing he was never much interested in horses, except as a means of following hounds, and for another he was revolted by the swindling and sharp practice that seemed inseparable from the sport. In all the novels there are only a few race-meetings—notably the meeting at Paris in the *Jaunts and Jollities* which is mostly taken up with the absurd foot race between Mr. Jorrocks and the Baron; the Grand Aristocratic steeplechase in *Mr. Sponge's Sporting Tour* when Jack Spraggon was killed: and the wholly ridiculous match in *Ask Mamma* between Cuddy Flintoff and Monsieur Jean Rougier.

"Racing," said Mr. Jorrocks, "is only for rogues! I never goes into Tat.'s on a bettin' day, but I says to myself as I looks at the crowd by the subscription-room door, 'there's a nice lot o' petty-larceny lads! I'd rayther be a black-faced chimley sweep nor a white-faced black leg!'"

Apart from his sporting pursuits, his frequent visits to Brighton and to Boulogne and his later journalism, we are thrown back almost entirely upon conjecture for his life in London, for he tells us little of it. He mentions that the year 1825 was a year of financial panic and uncertainty. (During the winter of 1825–26, no fewer than 770 banks stopped payment.) "It was," he says, "the great 'Bubble' year, when so many banks failed and so many preposterous schemes were broached. The railway mania was bad enough, but, being all directed to one object and that a legitimate one, presented nothing like the insanity of 1825." There had been no such frenzy of speculation since the days of Robert Walpole, when the South Sea Bubble swelled and broke, and a company was formed and fully subscribed "for an object which cannot at present be revealed to the public."

Even conjecture fails to give us any but the most meagre facts about his legal career, and he only mentions two dates—1825, when he was articled to Mr. William Bell, and 1828, when he was admitted in Chancery, being then in residence at Lincoln's Inn Fields. A comparison of the maps of London published in 1792 and 1824 shows that during the time that Surtees lived there the tide of building had flowed around Lincoln's Inn Fields, engulfing Whetstone's Park, which had bounded them on the north, and the open squares on the other sides. The famous Lincoln's Inn Fields Theatre, with its memories of John Gay and the first production of the *Beggar's Opera*, had gone long before, and the Sardinia Chapel—where Fanny Burney was married—had been destroyed by the Gordon Rioters. But on the whole London had not yet lost its connection with the countryside.

Finsbury, Kensington and Paddington, Hampstead and Highgate were still separate villages. The citizens of London could take their pleasure at week-ends and on summer evenings in hayfield and wood without going far from their doors. Harriers still met at Streatham, Dulwich, Southgate, Finchley, Hounslow and Sunbury. Women cried "Sweet lavender" and "Cherry ripe" in the West End streets, and nightly horse-drawn waggons rolled in to Covent Garden market with fruit and vegetables from Kent and Surrey. Maida Vale still justified its name and southward from it there was an almost continuous stretch of open country round Westbourne Green, Kensington, Earl's Court, Little Chelsea and so to the river Thames. In the West End itself the London Squares were coming into being, replacing the private gardens of the great houses that had once stood there. Even to-day there are few places in the West End from which, by looking in one direction or another, a man cannot see at least one tree. It must have seemed circumscribed and shut in to the boy fresh from the open country round Hamsterley : but at least he could mount his hack and in an hour or two be in the open country north of the Regent's Park, or following the hounds towards Streatham and Croydon. It is little wonder that the next few pages of his memoirs are so barren of legal information and so full of hunting. He was a countryman, and in 1825 it was not far from Lincoln's Inn Fields to the green heart of the country.

Hunting to-day is so exclusive and so expensive a sport that it is difficult to realize that in the late eighteenth and early nineteenth centuries it was as common and as popular as football. It is not surprising that this should have been so in the country, where nearly every great house had its private pack of hounds and where the smaller farmers' packs abounded ; where there was so little in the way of counter-attraction and where every man except the farm labourer kept some sort of horse that could be pulled out of trap or farm-cart to follow the hounds. Before the coming of the railways travel was difficult and costly and every rival community was a self-contained unit, finding its own pleasures, of which a pack of foxhounds or harriers was not the least. The pack often consisted of only a few couple of second-rate hounds, the field displayed every variety of mount from the nobleman's hunter to the tinker's donkey and every variety of dress from pink coat to moleskins. There were as often as not as many foot-followers as horsemen. But it is surprising to find the sport so generally popular in the towns. The Corporation of London kept their own hounds as did other great cities like Birmingham and Manchester, and on holidays the city merchants on horseback and their apprentices on foot turned out to follow them. Most notable and longest lived of the democratic packs was the Epping Hunt, which lasted until 1853 and numbered at one time three thousand horsemen, eight hundred vehicles and an army of foot-followers. This cavalcade followed the carted deer and owned a trusted favourite called "Mrs. Clarke," which could always be relied upon to give them a straight run and end up at the point at which they had already decided to dine.

The Industrial Revolution and the growth of the railways put an end to these popular packs. Labour began to move from the farms to the mills and towns, and the farmers, hard-pressed for help, had less time to think of hunting in the struggle to make a living. The railways cut across hunting country in every direction. The towns spread outwards into the countryside until the meet took place too far away for the man who had no means of transport to get there. Then too, as the railways became quicker and more efficient, men who could afford it found it pleasanter to journey by rail to a country where the hounds were good, the field well mounted and the sport less obstructed by vehicles and foot-followers. Men thought twice about hacking from the City to Croydon, there to take their chance of sport with the hare or the carted deer, when in an hour or two they and their horses could be conveyed in comfort to Leicestershire or Sussex. The emphasis on hunting began to be laid less on the hounds than the horses, less on the work in covert and the kill than on the gallop and the jump. Hunting as Surtees knew it began to give place to hunting as Nimrod liked it. It was becoming aristocratic again as it was under the Tudors and the Stuarts. Democratic hunting came in with the first George and went out with the fourth. Mr. Patrick Chalmers writes in his *History of Hunting*, " Among the changes which were, with the Georgian era, taking place in Society was the appearance on the hunting field of those whom a chronicler of the period calls ' the common people.' The common people are, of course, according to the supercilious ethics of the time, the merchants, the lawyers, the clergy, the medical men, and the middle classes generally." He quotes two cases of hunting merchants who were surely the ancestors of Mr. John Jorrocks, Grocer, Tea Dealer and M.F.H. Mr. Alderman Humphrey Parsons, brewer of " London Stout," hunted not only in England but at Fontainebleau with Louis XV's staghounds. He so much impressed Louis with his horsemanship that he secured the exclusive monopoly of " serving the French Nation with his Extract of Malt," thereby anticipating Mr. Jorrocks, who went into the " cut-'em-down countries " with his order book in his pocket and followed prospective customers up to but not over a fence, enquiring, " Did you say two chests o' black and one o' green ? " Forty years later there appeared John Cook, son of a corn chandler at Christchurch in Hampshire, who married a Surtees and wrote *Observations of Hunting*. Surtees must have known about him for family reasons, and it is evident that he had read the *Observations on Hunting*, for he borrows freely from it for the letters from

Mr. Puffington to Lord Scamperdale, and Richard Bragg to Benjamin Brick. There is a tradition, too, that the original Lucy Glitters was Squire Forester's hard-riding Miss Phoebe Higgs.

The reign of George IV was the heyday of the merchant sportsman and his field of activity was the area round London. Croydon was the headquarters, and every Saturday the merchant on his hunter, the butcher on his cob, the tinker on his donkey, hurried out in that direction to ride with any of the packs which met in that district to hunt the hare, the fox or the carted deer. A typical hunt was the Old Surrey, which appears so often in the columns of the *New Sporting Magazine* and which is immortalized in *Jorrocks's Jaunts and Jollities.* How truly this was a merchants' hunt is shown by the conversation at the meet described in "The Yorkshireman and the Surrey" which appeared in the *New Sporting* and was reprinted in the *Jaunts and Jollities.*

"A gentle breeze wafted divers scraps of conversation to his ear.

"What is that hound got by? No. How is that horse bred? No. What sport had you on Wednesday? No. Is it a likely find to-day? No, no, no; it was not *where the hounds*, but what *the consols*, left off at; what the four per cents., and not the four horses, were *up to*; what the condition of the money, not the horse, market. 'Anything doing in Danish bonds, sir?' said one. 'You must do it by lease and release, and levy a fine,' replied another. Scott *v.* Brown, *crim. con.*, to be heard by the Chief Justice on or before Wednesday next.—Barley thirty-two to forty-two. . . . Have you heard that Brown and Co. are in the *Gazette*? No, which Brown—not John Brown? No, William Brown. What, Brown of Goodman's Fields? No, Brown of —— of Street—Brown*e* with an *e*; you know the man I mean.—Oh! Lord, ay, the man wot used to be called *nosey* Browne.' A general move ensued, and they left 'the meet.'"

They had only a few more years ahead of them in the hunting field. Railways were ruining the country, the towns were spreading out into the fields and Mr. Dombey was replacing Mr. Jorrocks. But they lasted long enough for Surtees to hunt with them all, fox, hare and staghounds, to jeer at them in the *New Sporting Magazine*, to pillory them in the *Jaunts and Jollities*, to achieve the apotheosis of the sporting cockney in *Handley Cross.*

One effect of the growing exclusiveness of hunting was that women began to ride with the hounds again. The London packs had an exclusively male field, and it is evident throughout all the Surtees novels that a woman in the hunting field was a rarity and not a popular one. It had been common for women to hunt up to the end of Stuart times and after that in France. Even in England they still went out with the royal packs, for Mr. Alexander Pope remarks that "to eat Westphalia ham in a morning, to ride over hedges and ditches on borrowed hacks, to come home in the heat of the day with a fever and (what is worse) with a red mark on the forehead from an uneasy hat, all this may qualify them to make excellent wives for fox-hunters and to bear an abundance of ruddy-cheeked children."

In 1795 the Countess of Salisbury kept her own hounds at Hatfield, and she and her hunt servants rode in sky-blue coats, black collars, silver lapels and jockey caps. In the following year the best woman to hounds in England was Lady Lade, who began life as a kitchen wench, graduated as the mistress of Sixteen-String Jack the Highwayman, whose hanging she attended, and ended by marrying Sir John Lade, the Corinthian, who was part jockey, part stable-boy, part coachman and wholly rascal. That versatile and brilliant woman Lady Mary Wortley Montagu took to hunting at the age of sixty-four and hunted regularly for many years thereafter. Surtees himself mentions a Mrs. Russell who used to hunt at Brighton in a black beaver bonnet, a scarlet waist and a sky-blue shirt. But these were aristocrats. When the merchant or the country squire went out to hunt, his wife remained in the parlour or the still-room. The most fervent imagination refuses to contemplate the idea of Mrs. Jorrocks following the Old Surrey or the Handley Cross.

The reigns of George IV and William IV saw the gradual disappearance of the farmers' and tradesmens' hunts and the formation of the great subscription packs, as we know them to-day. The enormous increase in the subscription packs in this period is proved by "Cecil" in his *Records of the Chase*, first published in 1854. He estimates the number at the beginning of the nineteenth century at about twenty-five, whereas the list that he gives at the date of publication includes nearly a hundred.

From 1825 till 1828 most of Surtees' hunting was with the various packs within reach of London. Much of it must have seemed strange to him; but it was a good apprenticeship for a sporting novelist, for he learned to know every form of hunting—fox, deer and hare. It gave him the knowledge and background for his earliest literary work, the hunting papers in the *New Sporting Magazine*. Above all it gave him Mr. Jorrocks. While he was still a law student he had to work at, or at least to attend, the office, and his hunting was limited to Saturdays and holidays like that of any of the London merchants whom he ridiculed. It was not a type of hunting that he cared for, and his satire is savage and at times extravagant when he writes of it. But better days were in store for him. In 1828 he was admitted in Chancery. He had learned all the law that he was ever likely to know and he had little intention of using it. In the following year he began to hunt at Brighton.

II

Brighton's splendid time began on a September day in 1783, when the Prince Regent drove into the town to stay with his uncle, the Duke of Cumberland. It lasted till his death in 1830.

Surtees first knew Brighton in 1829 and wrote of it some years later. " In the first place," he wrote, " the Brighton I first knew was exclusive. If you didn't belong to the ' Set ' you couldn't get in. Now there are so many sets that the deuce is in it if a man doesn't light on his legs in some of them." But, he adds, " if I had my choice between the Brighton of the 'twenties and the Brighton of the present time, I would prefer the latter."

No doubt Brighton in 1829 was too exclusive for him. He was a great man at Hamsterley, but hardly of such standing as to be invited to the Pavilion in the last year of George's reign. He was in the hunting set and he met the Duke of Wellington in the hunting field. But the reigning set at Brighton was never predominantly sporting, though the Prince Regent hunted there and his entourage included Sir John Lade and Lord Onslow. During George's reign, and especially during his regency, the company at the Pavilion and in the Steyne was brilliant, intellectual and aristocratic. George IV himself left Brighton for good soon after 1823, so that the real period of its splendour covered exactly forty years. During that forty years almost every well-known historical figure passed across that gay stage—George himself, Mrs. Fitzherbert, Lady Conynghame and Lady Jersey ; the Duke of Wellington and Sir Hudson Lowe ; Charles James Fox, Sheridan, Rossini, William Pitt ; the Duc de Chartres and the unhappy Princesse de Lamballe.

Once Brighton's decline set in the process was rapid. It seemed to come suddenly after 1837. In that year Mrs. Fitzherbert, who had known it so long, died there. In the same year Queen Victoria, newly crowned, visited it, but found it noisy and decided never to enter it again. The railways completed the work of destruction. In 1841 the London and Brighton railway opened, and thereafter Brighton was submerged by a flood of those trippers whom Cobbett gracefully described as " human vermin."

Surtees knew and loved it from 1829 till 1838 when he returned to Hamsterley, though he visited it afterwards and died there in 1864. He must have been fond of it in the earlier days, for he devotes more space to it in his memoirs than to the whole of his previous life. Needless to say most of the memoirs are devoted to the hunting field. The Brookside Harriers and the South Down Foxhounds must have seemed like a vision of Paradise to him after the Cockney packs, and he hunted regularly with them both.

The Master of the South Down at that time was Colonel Windham, who controlled his pack by whistle. " A peculiar method," Surtees observed, " the like of which I have never seen before and have never seen since." The whistling was done by his huntsman Arbor, and the method must have impressed Surtees deeply, for it reappears in *Hawbuck Grange* in the person of Captain Cashbox of the Stout-as-Steel Hunt.

More important is the Baron Gablenz, a native of Saxony, who had come to England with the avowed intention of marrying an heiress. " You have nothing to do but tell the Baron that so-and-so had money and he would be at her in a moment." In this year of 1829 he was in pursuit of a young lady reputed to have £10,000 a year. He was in error, for the lady's £10,000 was capital and not income, but that did not discourage him. " Ah well," he remarked, " it will be ten thousand the first year at all events." If he heard of a man with money he was less interested, for " Vell, my good friend, vot for that to me ? I cannot go for to marry to him ! " But he never found his heiress, and in the early thirties he killed himself at Baden, after losing more than he could pay at cards.

All foreigners, especially Frenchmen, were funny to Surtees, who was nothing if not insular. His later experience of hunting at Boulogne and Samer deepened this view, and the crude Parisian humour of the *Jaunts and Jollities* is the expression of it. Baron Gablenz was not a Frenchman, but Surtees may be excused for finding him ridiculous. He was passionately fond of what he called " foxin' " and used to ride in the most extravagant costume. Surtees was always a stickler in the matter of dress in the hunting field, and Brighton was a place where dress meant much. The severe elegance of Mr. Brummell had replaced the flamboyance of the Prince Regent, and it is as well that Mr. Brummell was no longer there to see Baron Gablenz in " an uncommonly gay-coloured cut velvet evening vest with steel buttons that had been doing duty overnight at Almack's or elsewhere."

Surtees took him to task about it, but Gablenz exclaimed, " Oh ! by my word, Sortee, there is nothing too good for foxin' in ! " He was a bold and determined horseman and " rode in the most break-neck style at the most impracticable places, seldom if ever coming to grief."

Thirty years later—more than twenty years after his death—he appears again as Prince Pirouetteza in *Plain or Ringlets*. He is still extravagantly dressed, still looking for an heiress, still " foxin' " with Mr. Jessop's or the Duke of Tergiversation's hounds. But most important of all was the Master of Ceremonies of Brighton, Captain Eld, who survives in *Handley Cross*. " Eld had long held the honourable office of Arbiter Elegantium, as the newspapers used to designate the office : and his chief duty seemed to be watching the various coaches as they entered Brighton, running the newcomers to ground at their hotels or lodgings and then digging them out as it were with a highly glazed card, which bore the talismanical name 'Captain Eld, M.C.' printed on it . . . At each (of the libraries) lay a large red-backed book devoted to the receipt of subscriptions to the Captain's emoluments. In these books the recipients of the aforesaid cards were expected to enter their names and addresses with the much more interesting addition of One, one, opposite. They were then entitled to get what they could for their guinea, which might be briefly described by the little world ' Nil.' It was pleasant to see the Captain trotting about—first after the coaches, then shedding his cards and anon watching the results at the libraries." From the background of George IV's Brighton there canters towards us Captain Miserrimus Doleful, M.C., of the Handley Cross Spa, with his seedy hat and his old military coat, mounted on the lean, white Rosinante that " went up and down like a yard and an 'alf of pump water."

Surtees was enjoying a measure of liberty now. He had been admitted as a solicitor and felt that he had done all that was required of him in that way. Having time to spare he decided to broaden his experience by a little foreign travel, and in 1829 he was in Paris. His travels never took him farther afield, for on the way he chanced to stop at Boulogne and came across another form of hunting.

Mr. Jorrocks in clover

[HANDLEY CROSS]

The hounds that Surtees encountered on the Calais road out of Boulogne belonged to a Mr. Sackville Cresswell, a native of Wiltshire. " A gentleman," Surtees explains, " accustomed to his comforts of which a pack of hounds was one." He was " a portly elderly gentleman, dressed in a lavish-crowned hat, with a green frock-coat and top boots, riding a good-looking bay horse." But it was an odd form of hunting, because no one except Cresswell and his servant followed the hounds. Surtees, it need hardly be added, turned his horse and rode on with them.

Unfortunately Mr. Cresswell was rather too fond of his comforts, and a few days after this meeting he was arrested for debt and lodged in the Boulogne gaol, locally known as the Hotel d'Angleterre. Wishing to spare his hounds from the general wreck of his affairs, he generously presented them to Surtees and to a Colonel Charrittée. So Surtees at the age of twenty-four found himself, for the first time and rather to his surprise, a master of hounds. The beginning of his mastership was attended with some difficulty. The ex-master was in gaol, the sole hunt servant had bolted and the new masters found themselves in charge of a few couple of hounds of which they did not even know the names, a serious handicap for a master or huntsman as Mr. Jorrocks would have agreed. Indeed the whole organisation, being without huntsman, horses or kennel book, was not unlike the Handley Cross when Mr. Jorrocks took it over. But Surtees was equal to the occasion. Five couple at a time the hounds were conveyed into the gaol, where Mr. Cresswell named them, the whole ceremony being courteously attended by the gaoler. (" Made Bin call over the 'ounds by name," records Mr. Jorrocks in his journal, " double-thonging him when he made a mistake.)

The masters had surmounted the first difficulty. They knew the names of their hounds. The next thing was to find somewhere for the hounds to live. There was a brief experiment with an Englishman resident in Boulogne, but it was unsatisfactory and they were removed to a small wayside inn called the " Rose sans Epine " where an accommodating Frenchman offered to look after them and to give them, for a franc a head, three courses and dessert daily. " The first course," Surtees explains, " consisting of soup maigre or bouillon, the second of the bouillon itself and the third of damaged ship's biscuit or black bread. The dessert would most likely be a cuff or a kick for bad manners during the meal."

Things were beginning to take shape. The hounds were housed and fed. Surtees and Charrittée were to hunt them themselves and there was no need for hunt servants or hunt servants' horses. The last difficulty, and it proved to be an unexpectedly large one, was to find something to hunt. The hounds were not particular. They would hunt fox, deer, hare, rabbit or, if nothing better presented itself, a stray cat. But Surtees, fresh from the Brookside, decided first of all to try hare. There were some hares about, though nothing would stop the natives from shooting them for what seemed to Surtees the wholly inadequate reason that the hares were on their land and belonged to them.

The country round Boulogne was divided up into countless small-holdings, whose owners resented the hunt riding over them. In fact, Mr. Cresswell had already quarrelled with most of them for this reason, and during the first few days under the Surtees–Charrittée régime the hunt collected more summonses for trespass than hares. As this looked like making hare-hunting extremely expensive, they decided to abandon it and to turn their attention to fox, if only because there were plenty of foxes among the dunes on the sea-coast which belonged to nobody and which were worth nobody's while to shoot. It was better and cheaper than hare-hunting, but "the scent was bad, the riding dangerous and the sport so-so." And the foxes themselves, possibly because they were French, seemed to take no interest in the sport. They were large, fine-looking animals, but without speed or cunning and never managed to give the hounds a run. Nor could they ever be persuaded to leave the area of the dunes.

By this time the reputation of the pack had spread and several Englishmen who lived at Boulogne, usually for reasons of debt in their own country, turned out to hunt with them. Something must be done to show sport, and Surtees conceived the brilliant idea of appealing to Mr. George Templer of Stovey House, near Exeter, a master of dwarf foxhounds, something of an eccentric and the inventor of a system for training foxes. "The system in brief consisted of an enclosed fox-court, a low diet and frequent stirring-up with a pig-jobber's whip." Mr. Templer embraced with enthusiasm the idea of extending his training to the idle foxes of Boulogne and even came over in person to superintend it. A publican of the name of Joe Jenkins was engaged "not only to find the foxes but also to superintend their gymnastic exercises." And in the course of a very short time Jenkins had some "half-dozen, ruddy, well-coated, full-brushed, gentlemen roaming disconsolately about his back-yard, looking anxiously up every now and then into the old fishing net that overspread its area and prevented their escape." The experiment was a success, almost too much of a success, for one of the first of these athletic foxes led them through an orchard and a garden. The owner was furious, quite unjustifiably so it seemed to Surtees, who remarks severely that a French peasant hasn't the slightest notion of hunting. He had served under the great Napoleon and he defied the hunt with a besom. (But they ought to have had James Pigg there to offer to fight the proprietor, as he did when he landed in the melon-frame.) But Surtees was not to be withstood and he was beginning to understand the French character. For a reward of five francs the Napoleonic veteran willingly allowed them to search both his garden and his house, and in the house Mr. Templer found the fox, which had gone to earth under the counterpane of the old man's bed. It was hauled out and taken outside, and the hunt continued.

But the veteran, having pouched his five francs, had not finished with them. He related the sad story to the editor of the Boulogne paper *L'Annotateur Boulonnais*, who made it the text of a leading article. "Mm. Les Anglais," the editor wrote, "having assembled in great numbers 'sur le territoire d'Ostrohowe sans doute lancer leur renard,' were driven off by the police and galloped off to Slack, there to enlarge their detested animal: which fox, after passing by Wimille and Wacquinghen, sought refuge in the house of un vieillard octogenaire, whom the hounds 'animés par leur ardeur naturel' knocked down; also broke all the crockery and ate all the victuals in the place." The article concluded by calling on the authorities for aid and protection against such outrages in future.

"The favour," Surtees adds drily, "was accorded," and the gendarmes were ordered to attend upon the hunt and prevent the members of it from enlarging their reynards, the consequence of which measure was to make the chase more like Mr. Jorrocks's "image of war without its guilt," and to increase his estimate of its danger beyond his calculation of twenty-five per cent.

From that point onwards the story is pure farce. Whenever the hunt went out they were accompanied by mounted gendarmes, armed with swords and pistols. The country through which they were going to ride was picketed by dismounted *gardes-champêtres*, armed with short swords and dressed in cocked hats and blue uniform. "These," Surtees writes, "come upon the party unaware, popping out from behind stone walls or any sort of ambuscade that would cover them, and cutting the horseman's bridle reins before he was aware of their presence."

Surtees and Charrittée tried every trick to get rid of these pests. They lavishly advertised the time and place of their meets and then met elsewhere at a different time. They hunted drags with such a liberal use of aniseed that the pace was too fierce for the mounted gendarmes to keep up. But nothing would shake off the *gardes-champêtres*. "The order of the day," Surtees wrote in his memoirs, "was somewhat after this fashion. First went the fox, down wind with an open country and nothing to stop him. Then went certain irrestrainable sportsmen after the fox, much in the manner of certain gentlemen at a stag hunt. Then presently came the hounds, noisy and clamorous, but soon subdued by the pace when once on the scent of what Beckford would call an 'extravagantly stinking fox.' With them of course went the mounted field, and after these would come two or three gendarmes armed with pistols, swords and carbines, riding great, lumbering, long-tailed, black horses, who went as long as they could."

The situation is so rich in humour, so infinite in possibilities, that it is a wonder that Surtees never used it in one of his novels. Perhaps he felt that it was one of those situations which, while they obstinately persist in real life, are considered too incredible for fiction. But the picture of that race across the fields of the hounds, the pink coats of the hunt, the helmets and swords of the gendarmes stayed in his mind, to reappear thirty years later in *Hawbuck Grange*.

The Duke of Tergiversation was entertaining the Prince of Spankenhausen—another incarnation of Baron Gablenz—Mynheer Van Cled and "several other great Dutch swells," and ordered out a troop of the local yeomanry as guard of honour to escort them to the meet. But the guard's duty did not end there. They rode with swords drawn in the wake of the hunt. No experience of Surtees' was ever wasted.

His conviction of the essential ridiculousness of the French nation has its roots in the hunting at Boulogne. It was soon to be confirmed and deepened by his experience with the hounds at Samer, a little town about nine miles from Boulogne. Surtees and Charrittée, a trifle discouraged by the reception they had met with at Boulogne, had resolved to change the scene of their activities, and with this end in view they got permission from the Duc de Polignac, the Grand Veneur of Charles X of France, to hunt all the royal forests in the Samer district. They decided to ingratiate themselves with the inhabitants from the start and invited the more distinguished local residents to a grand hunt dinner at the Tête de Bœuf, the Samer Inn which was kept by a Monsieur Saurange, postmaster of the town and, as it turned out, the Master of the Samer Hunt, a pack of whose existence they had not then heard. The evening was a wild success. Surtees, on being informed of the existence of the Samer Hounds, instantly made them a present of two hounds of his own, Warrior, an incorrigible babbler and skirter, and Wonderful, "who would only do what he liked, which was generally nothing." "They were," says Surtees, "generously presented to the French pack with a due exordium on their merits." The French were overjoyed and, to cement the friendship, invited Surtees and Charrittée to bring their hounds to Samer for a "Grand Union Hunt" with their own pack. "The evening closed with so grand a debauch of Eau-de-vie that towards midnight Mr. Saurange was carried home on a shutter."

The day of the Grand Union Hunt arrived, but there was a slight mistake about the time. While the Englishmen still sat at breakfast in the Tête de Bœuf they heard a deafening noise outside the inn, a combination of horses' hooves, brass instruments and an occasional gun-shot. The French hunt had already left for the meet "armed with guns and carbines, playing on numerous twisted horns." Surtees and his friends mounted and rode in pursuit, following the sound of the horns and the guns. It was the practice of the Samer Hunt to put their hounds into coverts to drive out foxes, hares or rabbits while the *chasseurs* of the hunt stood with their guns at covert-side and blazed away at anything that might appear. Mr. Jorrocks's estimate of twenty-five per cent. of danger had gone up to an alarming figure. Surtees kept out of the way as well as he could and left early in the day after expressing profound gratitude for their hospitality and admiration for their sport. The last he saw of the Samer Hounds were Warrior and Wonderful having a private hunt of their own after some other quarry.

Once with the Samer Hounds was enough. They tried Boulogne once more, but during their absence at Samer, the crop of *procès verbaux* had reached maturity and judgments were ready for execution. Surtees did not wait for them. "All those who would not by doing so jump out of the frying-pan into the fire made off to England."

He landed at Dover just in time for the opening day of the season with Mr. Henry Oxenden's hounds in East Kent. He never hunted in France again, though he continued to visit it from time to time; and it is to a passport issued to him at Calais in August 1835 that we owe the only description that we have of his appearance as a young man.

Age	30 years (32?)
Height	6 feet 1 inch
Hair	Brown
Forehead	Wide
Eyes	Brown
Nose	Ordinary (Moyen)
Beard	Chestnut
Face	Oval
Girth	Average

When he returned from Boulogne he was twenty-four and another chapter of his life was finished. He had experimented with the Law and more or less abandoned it. He had hunted with the packs round London and Brighton, and at Boulogne and Samer. Hunting was always to be his first love, but he was ready now to look for a new career. He had always had " a taste for scribbling," and in the winter of 1829 he began to gratify it.

III

Some lives seem to fall naturally into divisions, and the year 1829 marked the distinct end of one period of Robert Surtees' life. Hamsterley and Ovingham were the first; London, Brighton and Boulogne the second. He had chosen his career and he was fortunate in it. He cared for two things, hunting and writing; and for the rest of his life he was to combine the two. Where most men's careers are forced upon them or come upon them by inheritance or chance so that they fret out their working lives under burdens that they hate, he was able to make a living—in so far as he needed to make a living—out of his pleasures. In nearly every way his was to be a life free from the ordinary cares and struggles, from financial anxiety and from insecurity of every sort. He was never to be one of those authors who do not know where their next meal or their next five-pound note is coming from. Inevitably this was to have its effect on his writing. What he was when he began to write at the age of twenty-four he remained to the end—a country gentleman, a hunting man, withdrawn and aloof from the turmoil of the world; satisfied with his own surroundings, a little intolerant and contemptuous of any other world than his own; incurious about the problems of his day, indifferent to social and industrial change, kindly, arrogant and obstinate. This, combined with a sense of humour that was often unkind and never subtle, was the equipment with which he began his literary career. Hamsterley and Ovingham had given him much—a settled background, a knowledge of sport, a strong and disciplined body. But beyond these they gave him that unquestioning self-assurance which is the result of a secure childhood, a leisurely education and an absence of financial strain. Strangely enough, he was inclined to be snobbish about his chosen profession of authorship. His own expression "a taste for scribbling" is illuminating. It may have been a casually modest way of referring to his talents, but as a rule he was neither casual nor modest. It seems more likely that in his inmost heart he felt that writing for profit was not a really fitting occupation for a man of his position. This is borne out by the fact that after his first book—*The Horseman's Manual*, a severely technical and legal work—he obstinately refused to sign any of his work. As a journalist he wrote under the name of "Nim South," out of compliment to a friend of his who was writing as "Nim North," and as a novelist he was always anonymous. He made his position perfectly clear about this in *Hawbuck Grange*. "We may say," he wrote, "with our excellent friend Peter Morris, that 'if putting our Christian name and surname at the beginning of a book were necessary conditions to the dignity of authorship, we should never be one while we live.' . . . We rejoice in the privilege of writing and printing *incognito*, and think with him that it is the 'finest discovery' that ever was made." He made an exception in favour of his first work, the full title of which is *The Horseman's Manual: On soundness and the Laws of Warranty and Generally on the Laws Relating to Horses*. Presumably his name as a lawyer and as a master of hounds would give weight to the book, and a technical treatise would rank above the comparatively low pursuit of writing fiction.

The book was published in 1831, so properly belongs to the next period of his life, but it does not form part of the canon of his literary work and may be briefly dismissed at this point. It has never been reprinted and to-day is hardly obtainable even by collectors. "It describes and considers," Mr. Cuming writes, "a number of cases which had come before the courts, gives judicial decisions, expert opinions and usages in connection with sale and purchase, privately and by auction. It has interest as being a literary link with Surtees' legal career—if it can be called a career." At any rate that career, for what it was worth, was over and the new life was beginning. It began inauspiciously and nearly perished at birth.

The winter of 1829 was a hard one, with much frost which seriously interfered with hunting. Surtees found himself at a loose end. The Law had lost for him whatever little attraction it had ever had, and his thoughts turned to "scribbling."

He began to work at a hunting novel, and when he had got about two-thirds of the way through it he showed it to two of his friends, who "so laughed it to scorn that I put it on the fire and half resolved to abandon the pursuit of letters for the future."

Most authors, or at any rate most young authors, know these candid friends. This particular pair, as it happened, did little harm, because they did not permanently discourage him; and upon them, whoever they were, there rests only the onus of the destruction of a manuscript by the greatest sporting novelist of that or any other day. Fortunately it was only half a resolve that he made. He resolved to take another and more expert opinion "of one of those best of all critics, a publisher." He had for some time kept a hunting journal, and from this he sketched out a few papers and offered them to Mr. Shury, the editor of the *Sporting Magazine*. "The bait took," he wrote, "and I was soon installed as first fiddle in the hunting line."

He was fortunate in the moment of his offer. Mr. Shury was "a very respectable and obliging man but without any sporting knowledge or authority." Up to that time the knowledge and authority had been supplied by Charles James Apperley, the famous Nimrod. But Nimrod had just fallen out with the proprietors of the *Sporting Magazine*. As a hunting correspondent he was without equal, and the magazine recognized it by paying him £1500 a year and maintaining six hunters for him. It was a princely salary for those days, but it was not enough for Nimrod, who was not avaricious but was so extravagant that sometimes he had to retire to Calais to escape his creditors. Nimrod demanded an increase of salary, which the magazine was unwilling or unable to pay. He withdrew to Calais and in 1830 Surtees was installed as hunting correspondent.

IV

It would be difficult to imagine two more different types than Nimrod and Surtees—different in temperament, in outlook, in education; different in speech and thought and writing. For six years Nimrod had been chief hunting correspondent to the *Sporting Magazine*, and when Surtees succeeded him in 1830 there began that rather senseless and intermittent squabble that lasted till Nimrod's death in 1843, only a few months after Surtees' last and most spiteful attack on him in *Handley Cross* in the famous Pomponius Ego episode. It is perhaps hardly fair to describe it as a "squabble," since all the animosity was on Surtees' side and Nimrod never attacked him or tried very hard to defend himself. They met from time to time on reasonably friendly terms and Nimrod was invited to stay at Hamsterley for the hunting. He and Surtees hunted together with Sir Matthew White Ridley's hounds, when Surtees perpetrated one of those hoaxes which seemed so diverting to the nineteenth century and seem so tedious to the twentieth. They fell out once or twice by correspondence, mostly over trivial details. Nimrod offered an article to the first number of the *New Sporting*, but Surtees would not accept it until he had seen it in draft. On another occasion Nimrod complained that an article had been published without the proof having been submitted to him. Nimrod wanted to be appointed hunting correspondent to the *New Sporting*, but Surtees, who had already acquired a taste for the work while with the "Old" *Sporting Magazine*, not unnaturally wished to be his own correspondent. There was no ill-feeling about it and most of their correspondence was friendly throughout the thirteen years of their association.

It is evident that on Nimrod's side at any rate there was no animosity. Yet Surtees from time to time mocked him in print in a way that surpasses the permissible limits of satire. The weapons of the satirist are surely the rapier and the poignard—the thought of Nimrod always seemed to impel Surtees to reach for the half-brick. The first of these attacks was in the *New Sporting Magazine* in the article "The Swell and the Surrey" which was later reprinted in *Jorrocks's Jaunts and Jollities*. Nimrod is not mentioned by name as he is on other occasions, but he is traditionally the object of the satire and an even more tolerant man than he might have objected to the description. "He is just turned out of the hands of his valet, and presents the very *beau ideal* of his caste—'quite the lady,' in fact. His hat is stuck on one side, displaying a profusion of well-waxed ringlets, a corresponding infinity of whisker, terminating at the chin, there joins an enormous pair of moustaches, which give him the appearance of having caught the fox himself and stuck its brush below his nose. His neck is very stiff; and the exact Jackson-like fit of his coat, which almost nips him in two at the waist, and his superlatively well-cleaned leather Andersons, together with the perfume and

Mr. Jorrocks's Lecture on "Unting."

the general puppyism of his appearance proclaim that he is a ' swell ' of the very first water, and one that a Surrey Sportsman would like to buy at his own price and sell at the other's." In a later article reprinted as " Mr. Jorrocks's Dinner Party " he appears by name as Mr. H'Apperley Nimrod and makes a speech in an unkind but by no means exaggerated parody of his real style. Nimrod's father had been a classical scholar, and he himself had learned Greek and Latin at Rugby. He was in truth a great deal too fond of interpolating classical allusions and Latin tags into his writing—a habit which never failed to annoy Surtees, who regarded it as pure affectation and was himself incapable of it. In one article in the *Quarterly*, Nimrod managed to introduce " Lycurgus, the Spartans, the Persians, and Ancient Greeks with a touch of Xenophon, Alexander the Great, Ulysses, Hannibal, Ralph Lambton, Osbaldeston, Cicero and I don't know who besides," Surtees remarks disgustedly. This article is parodied in Mr. O'Dicey's speech at the " Ordinary " dinner in *Plain or Ringlets*

Nimrod's speech at " Mr. Jorrocks's Dinner Party " is not an unfair imitation if a little unkind. At any rate his speech compares favourably with that of Mr. Jorrocks himself, which consisted largely of hiccups, and with that of Mr. Crane, the wine merchant, whose peroration was, " Gentlemen, I will not trespass longer upon your valuable time, but as you seem to enjoy this wine of my friend Mr. Jorrocks, I may just say that I have got some more of the same quality left, at from forty-two to forty-eight shillings a dozen, also some good stout draught-port, at ten and sixpence a gallon—some ditto werry superior at fifteen ; also foreign and British spirits, and Dutch liqueurs, rich and rare."

There are various manuscript notes among Surtees' private papers for further variations on the Nimrod theme, which were apparently never written or never published, and in the first serial edition of *Handley Cross*, Nimrod gives evidence before the Commissioners of Lunacy. But the Pomponius Ego day is left in, and it is the last and most unkind jeer of all. Yet it is not wholly unfair. Nimrod was a brilliant hunting correspondent, a superb horseman and a pleasant person, but he had his faults. He was flamboyant and self-satisfied, his classical education was obtrusive and he was a tuft-hunting snob of the most blatant type, in all of which qualities he was exactly the opposite of Surtees. When out hunting he looked first at the field, next at the horses and last of all at the hounds, while to Surtees the hounds were everything. But with all his exuberance and display he was a really good writer—his *Life of John Mytton* is one of the classics of sporting literature—and he enjoyed enormous success. Perhaps that irked Surtees a little. He was human enough to feel jealousy, and he was not to know success himself for many years.

The *Sporting Magazine* had another hunting correspondent, a Mr. Copland, who wrote under the name of "Dashwood." But Copland lived at Worthing and confined his attention to the doings of Colonel Wyndham and the South Down Foxhounds. Even so, he was always late with his copy. So Surtees really had the field to himself. His first paper, "Breaking Ground," appeared in the *Sporting Magazine* in February 1830 and his last in January 1831. He seems to have been appointed chief hunting correspondent towards the end of the 1830 season and he contributed articles on the Brighton Harriers and the Boulogne and Samer Hounds. The account of the run with the Brighton Harriers appeared in May and was the first to be signed with his pseudonym of "Nim South." The others were either anonymous or by "A Durham Sportsman." At the beginning of the season of 1831 he was regularly employed as hunting correspondent and toured in Sussex, Warwickshire and Leicestershire. It would be interesting to know what salary or remuneration he received, but he makes no mention of it. It is, however, evident by the end of 1830 that he was finding it a much more expensive occupation than he had bargained for.

"None save those who have tried it," he wrote, "can have any idea of the enormous cost of hunting touring. Everybody thinks that a red coat is a fair subject to plunder. The four-and-twenty shillings and sixpence a week of the livery-stable keeper is bad enough to the man who knows what horses cost in their own stables, but the 24/6d of the livery man sinks into insignificance beside other exactions."

He had an idea of buying a share in the magazine, and so exercising some control over its management; and the feeling of being a salaried man was not congenial to him. The breach came in February 1831, when he wrote to the editor proposing an arrangement whereby he would receive an interest in the magazine sufficient to cover his hunting expenses together with a proportionate share in the profit, with the option on ceasing to write of buying such a share at a valuation. The idea did not commend itself to the proprietors, who instructed the editor to inform him that they "respectfully but firmly declined admitting any gentleman, however talented, to a share in the magazine." "The Proprietors," the editor added, "were perfectly aware of the value of his services" and were willing to make an offer "greater than any the Proprietors ever intended to make and more than under any circumstances would ever be made to any other gentleman."

More it might have been, but it was not enough for Robert Surtees, who in any case was never prepared either to bargain or to compromise. In February he severed his connection with the *Sporting Magazine* and began to look round for new activities.

He had not far to look. He had recently met Rudolph Ackermann, and the association with the family began which lasted till the publication of Surtees' *Analysis of the Hunting Field* in 1846.

Ackermann was a German from Stolberg, in the Saxon Horz. He had been apprenticed to his father as a coach-builder in his native town, but soon left to visit Dresden and other German towns and Paris, from where he went on to London. There he settled down as a coach-designer, among his products being the Lord-Lieutenant of Ireland's coach in 1790 which cost £7000 and the hearse for Lord Nelson's funeral in 1805. But coach-designing was only one of his many talents. He managed an art school, opened a factory at Chelsea for water-proofing leather and cloth, experimented on balloons, and was almost the first man in London to use gas for lighting his business premises. But his real interest lay in book illustration and coloured prints, and his print shop at 96 Strand was world-famous. The elder Ackermann had a stroke in 1830 which prevented him from attending to his business, which was thereafter carried on by his son Rudolph Ackermann, junior, the father dying in 1834. The importance of the Ackermann family to the history of book illustration in England can hardly be over-estimated and their addiction to coloured sporting prints was of the utmost value to authors such as Nimrod and Surtees, and to artists such as John Leech, Henry Alken and Talbot K. Brown.

In the year 1831 Ackermann and Surtees went into partnership. With Ackermann as printer and publisher, and with Surtees as editor and hunting correspondent they started the *New Sporting Magazine*.

CHAPTER III

Into Covert

" Now let your huntsman throw in his hounds as quietly as he can, and let two whippers-in keep wide of him on either side . . . Now, if you can keep your brother-sportsmen in order, and put any discretion into them, you are in luck : they more frequently do harm than good."—Peter Beckford.

" 'Osses 'eads turn one way, th' 'ounds brisk up at the move, the coffee-room breaks up, frinds pair off to carry out jokes, while the foot people fly to the 'ills, and the bald-'eaded keeper stands 'at in 'and at the gate to let th' 'ounds into covert."—*Handley Cross.*

I

Surtees' parting with the " Old " *Sporting Magazine* was fairly friendly, but his actions during the next few months were the very opposite. Granted that a new venture must fight for its existence, granted that it must compete deliberately and fiercely with its predecessor, granted, too, the inevitability of certain contributors leaving the old and joining the new—granted all this, it is still difficult not to feel that Surtees' attitude towards the " Old " *Sporting* went very near the limits of fair competition and showed how pugnacious he could be. His memoirs record one after another the list of contributors whom he attracted from the " Old " to the *New Sporting*, and he chronicles them in a gleeful manner that shows that his own acquisitions meant even less to him than their loss. All was fish that came to his net at the start—even fish like Dashwood, whom he did not particularly want, thought little of and eventually got rid of.

Dashwood, the hunting correspondent who lived at Worthing, was the first to secede—" who," Surtees writes, " if he did not strengthen us much at all events weakened them." After him " came Dicky Lawrence, the veterinary author, of whom the same may be said." But for a time Lawrence was very useful. His versatility enabled him to contribute articles on such various subjects as hunting, anatomy, veterinary surgery and the current exhibition at the Royal Academy. He was useful again some years later when he published a small volume in imitation of Swift's directions to domestic servants. It contained some pages of advice to young horsemen which Surtees used almost without alteration and quite without acknowledgment in one of Mr. Jorrocks's " Sportin' Lectors " in *Handley Cross*.

He was even more successful in luring artists away from the " Old " *Sporting*. " The great blow to the ' Old ' *Sporting Magazine*," he notes, " was getting the celebrated Royal Academician, Abraham Cooper, away from them. He had long superintended the engraving and contributed largely to the illustration of the work. Cooper was a sportsman and an artist, self-taught, combined. . . . Cooper brought with him not only some of the first artists but some of the first engravers of the day." J. F. Herring was one of the more important recruits that Cooper brought in, and he was followed by Henry Bernard Chalon, who exhibited nearly two hundred pictures at the Academy between 1792 and 1847, and Sir Edwin Landseer, whose drawings Surtees courteously but perhaps not unjustly describes as " mere make-weights for the sake of the name : ' The Pig and a Nondescript ' and ' A Goat '—not very sporting animals, any of them." But besides these, Landseer contributed three paintings : " Dead Red Deer," " Trim, a celebrated Spaniel " and " Deerstalking." Francis Grant, who later became President of the Royal Academy, was a friend of Surtees and contributed regularly from the very earliest days. They are all mentioned later by Mr. Ruddle, the artist in *Young Tom Hall* the unfinished novel of the year 1851.

Sporting prints and pictures had for years been one of the traditions of the house of Ackermann, who were publishing the magazine.

Surtees can hardly be blamed for stealing Nimrod from the " Old " *Sporting*, as Nimrod had already fallen out with them. In fact Nimrod first approached Surtees in April 1831, making him an offer of some papers which Surtees did not immediately accept. Nimrod, of course, was anxious for a salaried appointment as chief hunting correspondent to the *New Sporting*, but as Surtees remarked, " with a taste for touring myself and the experience of the ' Old ' magazine before our eyes, we were not likely to set up Nimrod with his half-dozen horses as they had done." But he was fully alive to the importance of securing the most famous hunting correspondent of his day, and was only slightly deterred by the fact that Nimrod had bound himself not to write on sporting subjects for any but the " Old " *Sporting* for a term of years. They got over the difficulty by the ingenious, but not entirely honourable, subterfuge of publishing Nimrod's articles anonymously in the *New Sporting*. But his style and his material were unmistakable, and before long even the pretence of anonymity was abandoned and the " Hunting Reminiscences, or the The Crack Riders of England " and the " Noctes Nimrodianæ " were among the most popular features of the magazine. And in 1834 they began to publish, though not without some hesitation on Surtees' part, Nimrod's " Life of John Mytton." Nimrod, it need hardly be said, was quite conscious of his own importance as a writer. " My name in the market is now good," he wrote, " and I do not arrogate too much when I assert that the time is approaching when it will be better," adding characteristically, " Consciousness of merit is inseparable from the possession of it." Surtees, though he would never have said it, was quite of the same opinion, and though Nimrod continued to angle for the appointment as hunting correspondent, he was quite determined to keep it in his own hands. But he continued to publish Nimrod, to hunt with him and maintain personally pleasant relations with him, to bicker with him over trifles and on every possible occasion to jeer at him in print.

Nimrod occasionally wrote on racing, though he admitted in volume four of the *New Sporting* that " no man cared less about racing than he did, and that every year that passed over his head made him care less." Having to write an article on racing, he wrote to the *New Sporting* asking them to send him all the back numbers of the *Racing Calendar*, which Surtees reckoned " could not have been had on the spur of the moment under £40 or £50." Racing was one of the few things that Surtees agreed with Nimrod about and he declined the expenditure. " To do him justice," he remarked, " Nimrod had no idea of not having anything he wanted, and this, too, regardless of expense." Surtees' temperament was different in this as in so many other ways. There was always in him a streak of dour north-country sense about money matters, without any trace of meanness. In later years, when he became High Sheriff of the County of Durham, he proposed and carried through some sensible and necessary reductions in the expenses attached to the office. So Nimrod had to do without his *Racing Calendar*. He very seldom wrote about racing, because he did not care about it and because the racing side of the paper was capably covered by a Mr. Hamilton Reynolds, an authority on his subject, but an idle man who, like Dashwood, seldom had his copy ready when the magazine was due to go to press. " I shall never forget," Surtees wrote, " seeing his MS. arrive at the printers at the last moment : it would be delivered in the most extraordinary state of confusion—scribbled on letter backs, old play-bills, anything he could get hold of—written in a hand that seemed impossible to decipher. After several attempts to read it I was obliged to give it to the printer, with, I confess, no great expectation of its merit." He always hoped to secure, but never succeeded in securing, as racing correspondent Mr. Ruff, the best-known living writer on racing and the founder of the famous *Ruff's Guide to the Turf*.

The *New Sporting*, being a new venture, could not afford at first a large staff, and Surtees had a profound belief in amateur correspondents for a sporting journal. His expressed opinion was that hunting- and shooting-men are generally well-to-do and can afford to disregard the small fees which a magazine of that type can pay. It is a strange opinion coming from one who had fallen out with his previous employers over the question of remuneration and who was later most successfully to haggle with his publishers over the terms for *Handley Cross*. No doubt there was something in it of that meanness that drives all employers to get as much out of their servants for as little as possible. But principally it came from that feeling of his that writing for money is really one of the things that a gentleman does not do. His passion for anonymity springs from the same source, as does that instinct which led him to keep his novels out of sight of his daughters, so that one of them said in later years that they had never read them because "Papa said there was nothing worse for young people than reading bad literature." But perhaps they were allowed to read his only signed work, *The Horseman's Manual*.

In the course of his quest for unpaid contributors, Surtees wrote to Hogg, the Ettrick Shepherd, asking him to contribute some articles on fishing, a request which sorely puzzled Hogg, who had never heard of that particular Robert Surtees or of any *Sporting Magazine*, "New" or "Old." "But if," he wrote, "you are either my old friend Mainsforth or any near relation of his, I will write for you for nothing with all the pleasure in the world. Otherwise," he adds in a sentence which all authors should honour, "I always take pay and will warrant any man an ass who doesn't." There is an echo of Hogg in *Handley Cross*, for he is reputed once to have said, "If I had fifty servants, they would all be lasses." "Women waiters agin the world, say I!" observed Mr. Jorrocks to Mrs. Muleygrubs. "I'll back our Batsay, big and 'ippy as she is, to beat any two fellers at waitin'." "Besides, you never see a bosky Batsay waiter, which is more than can be said of all dog un's."

One of the most successful amateur contributors was Mark Lemon, who wrote semi-sporting sketches under the name of "Tom Moody" and who later became editor of *Punch*, in which capacity he refused the manuscript of that most unlucky novel, *Young Tom Hall, his Heartbreaks and Horses.* One of the most trying was a Mr. Young who had a passion for cock-fighting. He was determined to interest Surtees in this, and arranged a rendezvous in a decaying house in a shabby neighbourhood south of the Thames. From this he refused to emerge or even to open the door until Surtees, after hurling pebbles through the window, was able to convince him that he was not a creditor or a bailiff. Young was convinced that cock-fighting was coming into fashion again, but Surtees had from the first set his face against what he considered the cruel blood-sports. He had never forgotten the scenes in the dog-fight pits of the East End, and in the *New Sporting* prospectus it had been laid down that all reference to such sports was to be excluded from their paper. " But," says Surtees, " it was cock, cock, cock, nothing but cock with him. So at length I was obliged to leave him to crow by himself." There was also a " very merry writer who, under the signature of 'Peter Prig,' had contributed some very amusing papers on foreign matters and fox-hunting at Tours." His real name was Jonathan Ball, and he appears in the *Jaunts and Jollities* as Ball, " one of these lads who can go in 'The Swell and the Surrey.' "

But the principal contributor to the *New Sporting Magazine* was the editor, Surtees himself, and his hunting tours were a regular and main feature of every number. Nimrod confined himself mostly to the great runs and great characters of the past. He was living for the most part at Calais and out of touch with contemporary hunting. This connection Surtees took on his own shoulders. He had acquired a taste for hunting correspondence while he was still with the " Old " *Sporting*. Now that he was editor of the " New " he had both the opportunity and the means of gratifying it.

For the first few months he was not alone as hunting correspondent, for Dashwood still lingered on, living at Worthing and confining his attention to the Sussex packs and to Goodwood Races. He reported these for the last time in 1831, and the following year Surtees did it himself. He was not a racing man, but he had never been to Goodwood and wanted to see it. Also he calculated that his expenses would amount to less than Dashwood's fee. But in fact Dashwood had outlived his usefulness, which had never been very great. Living in Sussex and being reluctant to go out of it restricted his activities, and he was always late with his copy and often failed to fill the pages allotted to him in the magazine.

Surtees wrote to him and asked if he still wished to be regarded as their correspondent, there was some acrimonious correspondence and Surtees discharged him. Dashwood chose to regard himself as unjustly treated and published a peevish pamphlet denouncing Surtees, who, always ready for a fight, reprinted it in the *New Sporting* with some scathing editorial notes in which he described Dashwood as "that silly, self-sufficient gentleman."

For a lawyer he had a gay disregard for the law of libel and before long it got him into trouble.

In the course of his hunting tours he often visited Warwickshire. He stayed with his friend Mr. Herbert Langham at Cottesbrooke Park in Northamptonshire and hunted with the Pytchley, and they decided for a change to go into Warwickshire and have a few days with Mr. Thornhill's Warwickshire Hounds. For their headquarters they selected Leamington, where there were then three main hotels—the Royal, the Regent and the Bedford. Having had previous experience of the Royal, where they had discovered that the port decanters held only three-quarters of a bottle, they put up at the Bedford, which was then kept by a Mr. Gumm. Surtees' opinion was printed in the *New Sporting Magazine* in the spring of 1824.

"Leamington," he wrote, "though not overflowing with company, boasts a fair sprinkling of sportsmen this year—more perhaps than any other quarter save Melton. Still the hotels are empty—or nearly so—in which state they are likely to continue. The Regent, which makes up about 150 beds, has about half a dozen single gentlemen in the house, and Copp's the Royal—of equal size—not many more. As to the Bedford, *by Gumm*, no one should think of going there who has not a hardy constitution and a long purse: and the large hotels are too numerous and too empty to spare many guests for the small ones. Still we can hardly say that we are sorry for the innkeepers, for there certainly never were a more rapacious set gathered together, as every person that has ever had any dealings with them can testify. Their delinquencies have led to the formation of a club."

Surtees was never in the habit of mincing his words, and, while the other Leamington hotel wisely ignored the attack, Mr. Gumm of the Bedford was stung into action. A plea for Mr. Gumm was entered not against Surtees but, as the law then went, against Ackermann, the printer; with damages for £500, subsequently amended by the judge's permission to £1000.

The plea is described by Surtees as a farrago of nonsense. In it Gumm is described as " a good, honest, servant of the Realm, who as such has always behaved and conducted himself and has always been reported, esteemed and accepted by and amongst his neighbours and other good and worthy subjects of the Realm to be a person of good name, fame and credit to wit in the County of Warwickshire. He carried on the trade and business of an innkeeper and has always behaved and conducted himself as such innkeeper with integrity and honesty and had not been guilty of making any extravagant or exorbitant charges or of any rapacious dealing or other misconduct in the course of his said trade." Finally Mr. Gumm was " daily and honestly acquiring in the way of his said trade or business divers great gains and profits to the great increase of his riches to wit in the County aforesaid." Ackermann, the unfortunate printer, " who," Surtees said, " in reality knew no more of the contents of each number before the Magazine was laid on his counter on publication day than did the man in the moon," was described as, " well knowing the premises but greatly envying the happy estate and conditions of the said plaintiff, and contriving wickedly and maliciously intending to injure the said plaintiff in his said good name, fame and credit. He falsely, wickedly and maliciously did compose and publish a certain false scandalous, malicious and defamatory libel of and concerning the said plaintiff, in the way of his said trade or business so carried on by him as aforesaid."

Counsel for the *New Sporting Magazine* was Mr. Matthew Davenport Hill, M.P., and the case came before the Lord Chief Justice and a special jury. Mr. Hill's speech was one of the wittiest and cleverest ever heard in a court of law and, according to Surtees, was interrupted time and again by roars of laughter in which the Lord Chief Justice himself joined. But in spite of his mirth he summed up against the magazine ; and the jury found for the plaintiff, contemptuously assessing the damages at one farthing. Surtees of course reported the case in the *New Sporting*, printed Mr. Hill's speech in full and ended up with a balance sheet of the action as in his opinion it affected the magazine :

	£	s.	d.
By one copy of the *New Sporting Magazine* sold to Mr. Gumm's Solicitor	0	2	6
To damages	0	0	0¼
Profit to *N.S.M.* proprietor.	0	2	5¾

As a hunting correspondent, Surtees was indefatigable. Besides Warwickshire he visited Cheshire, Dorset, Sussex, Northamptonshire, Surrey and Leicestershire, and he reported racing at Goodwood and in Paris. However some of his other correspondents may have failed to fill the space allotted to them, he took his fair share of the work of filling the paper and more than his share. As early as the third number of the magazine in the summer of 1831 he began to chronicle the doings of John Jorrocks of Great Coram Street, Grocer and Tea Dealer of St. Botolph's Lane in the City of London. It was this series which was subsequently reprinted as *Jorrocks's Jaunts and Jollities* and became the first part of the Jorrocks Trilogy.

" The most useful man to the work," Surtees wrote later, " beyond all question, though I say it who perhaps should not, was Mr. Jorrocks, the sporting grocer of Great Coram Street, who not only followed all legitimate field sports, but indulged in diverse vagaries not connected therewith. Jorrocks could turn his hand to almost anything. He made his début," he continues, " in the third number of the work, in ' The Day with the Surrey,' precisely as the original made it to me out hunting with those hounds." It would be intensely interesting to know who was the original of that great figure, but Surtees never disclosed his identity and we only know that the original of Leech's drawings, which did so much to make Mr. Jorrocks widely known, was Nicholls, a coachman whom he sketched during a service in church

Mr. Jorrocks came into being in 1831, and for the the next fourteen years he was never long absent from his creator's mind. From July 1831 to September 1834 he riots through the pages of the *New Sporting Magazine*, hunting, shooting, racing, masquerading as a French colonel and, as ever, revelling in good food and good drink. In 1838 these papers were collected and published in book form as *Jorrocks's Jaunts and Jollities, or the Hunting, Shooting, Racing, Driving, Sailing, Eating, Eccentric and Extravagant Exploits of that Renowned Sporting Citizen, Mr. John Jorrocks of St. Botolph's Lane and Great Coram Street*. The preface states that, " The popularity which then (in the *New Sporting*) attended them induces the author to hope that in their present revised form, they may meet with the approbation of the general reader." It was published in 1838 by Walter Spiers of 399 Oxford Street with twelve uncoloured illustrations by " Phiz " (Hablot K. Browne), and a second edition was published in the following year. A third edition was published in 1843 by Rudolph Ackermann with fifteen coloured plates by

Henry Alken. In the same year Mr. Jorrocks reappears in *Handley Cross*, the greatest work of the Trilogy and in Surtees' own opinion "the best thing I have ever written."

This view was not shared by Colburn, the publisher, who urged Surtees to cut Jorrocks out of the book altogether. Strange as it may seem to-day, Jorrocks at that time was considered coarse, and Colburn was hesitant about publishing the book at all. His literary adviser, William Sholbert, concurred in the opinion and made certain suggestions for its amendment.

> " (1) Put name to work.
> (2) Attend to Mr. C's suggestions for improving and curtailing the work.
> (3) The story meagre. Prune down a little of the coarseness of the fox-hunting grocer."

There was trouble too about the title. The work had already run as a serial through the *New Sporting*, beginning under the name of "The Gin and Water Hunt," which was changed after the first few numbers. In the correspondence between Colburn and Surtees and in the original agreement it is referred to as the "Handycross Hounds," or "a suitable title to be mutually agreed upon." While this agreement was being discussed, Surtees, that stout supporter of amateur writers unless he happened to be the writer in question, objected strenuously to a clause that gave the publisher the right to deduct five per cent. for bad debts and a further five per cent. for office expenses before the author received his half-share of the profits. After some argument Colburn gave way and the clause was deleted from the agreement. The first edition was in three volumes—without illustrations—but was not a success. Colburn had printed 6000 copies of the first part, but was left with over 2000 on his hands and printed only 4000 of the second and third. The next edition was issued in seventeen monthly parts, beginning in March 1853, with illustrations by John Leech. It was republished again with Leech's illustrations in 1854 and this edition was more profitable. *Mr. Sponge's Sporting Tour*, Surtees' first real success, had come out the year before, and this helped the sales of *Handley Cross*. Even so they were not startling, and as late as 1858 Surtees could write, "I believe it was paying something, at all events it was out of debt last summer."

The third book of the Jorrocks Trilogy, *Hillingdon Hall*, appeared in the *New Sporting* from February 1843 to June 1844, when it ended

"'Ow are ye all?"

[HANDLEY CROSS]

abruptly at Chapter XXII. There were seven uncoloured plates, four by Wildrake and three by H. Heath. Colburn published it in three volumes without illustrations in 1845. It was an almost total failure, which is hardly surprising. It is the weakest of the three and its predecessors had not had enough success to carry it on their backs; also it was published too early to share in the reflected glory of *Mr. Sponge*.

Mr. Jorrocks's life from his beginning in the *New Sporting* to the end in *Hillingdon Hall* covers a period of fourteen years. And during these years there had been a change in Surtees' life. In 1831, when the story began, he was living in London and editing the *New Sporting Magazine*. In 1841, when it ended, he was back at Hamsterley for good, and not only back there but owning it. His father, mother and elder brother had died. He had started a pack of hounds and given it up, had married and become a Justice of the Peace and Deputy Lieutenant.

Surtees was editor of the *New Sporting* for five years, and later he remarked that " Editing is very good fun—for a time." There is some uncertainty as to his reasons for giving up the work and it is possible that he quarrelled with Ackermann. Certainly there was some dissension between them, for a letter exists from Ackermann to Surtees, dated 19th April 1843, in which he regrets that there has been a little difference between them during the last few years. " I do hope and trust," he goes on, " you will overlook it and not think anything more about it, as anything I can do to merit your approbation in the future will give me the greatest pleasure." It is clear that not only was there dissension but that Ackermann was, or thought he was, in the wrong, but there are no further details extant which would enable us to relate this to the parting with the *New Sporting*. It is possible that it refers to Ackermann's action in 1838 in undertaking the publishing of a rival journal, the *Sporting Review*, which Surtees resented the more for the fact that its editor was Mr. J. W. Carleton, whom he hated and with whom he once wanted to fight a duel. All we can say with certainty is that relations between Surtees and Ackermann were strained and that Ackermann did his best to effect a reconciliation. In Surtees' " Farewell," published in the issue of December 1836, no reference of course is made to any such trouble and he gives as his reason for resigning the fact that " for some time past circumstances have prevented our giving the work the attention which it requires."

This is probably no more than the truth. His elder brother, Anthony, had died of smallpox in 1831 and Surtees was heir to Hamsterley. We know, from all the evidence of his later life, that he took this duty seriously and he must have found it difficult to reconcile his editorial and touring duties with the necessary visits to Hamsterley. He visited it as often as he could, and it is during this period that he entertained Nimrod there and hunted with him with Sir Matthew White Ridley's Hounds. There were other things, too, that drew him back to Hamsterley. His mother was in failing health and in fact died the year after he resigned, his father surviving her only by one year. He was being urged to stand for Parliament and accepted nomination as Conservative candidate for Gateshead at the 1837 election.

In 1836 the *New Sporting* was advertised for sale. " The *New Sporting Magazine*," the advertisement ran, " was established by gentlemen who carried it on more for amusement than profit, consequently it has not attained the circulation it is capable of. It has, however, been steadily increasing without the aid of advertising and the gross receipts are now about £2000 a year : and it will be sold at such a price as will yield a very large profit on the present circulation." But no buyer came forward and the Magazine continued under the editorship of George Tattersall, better known as an illustrator under the name of " Wildrake." Surtees kept his interest in it and wrote for it occasionally, and both *Handley Cross* and *Hillingdon Hall* ran through it as serials. But it never made a reasonable profit, and in 1846 it was absorbed by the *Sporting Review* which in its turn was absorbed by the " Old " *Sporting Magazine* in 1848. There is a certain grim justice in the fact that the " Old " *Sporting*, from which Surtees broke away and which he did his best to injure, should in the end have survived and absorbed its rival and would-be supplanter.

Surtees' resignation of his editorship marks the end of another distinct period of his life. In the first period he had chosen his career. In the second he made his early experiments, found his strength and his line of country, accumulated experience and mastered his technique. The beginning of the third period finds him established as an author and entering on the long series of sporting novels on which his fame rests. It finds in existence Mr. Jorrocks, that truly great comic character, certainly the best-known and most loved of all his characters. But above all it finds him returning to Hamsterley. Writing was to be his career ; but Hamsterley was his life. There is abundant evidence in his later memoirs and correspondence that as such he regarded it. Writing, he seems to have felt, was all very well, an agreeable hobby and not an unprofitable one. But what he was born for was the life of Hamsterley, to hunt his own hounds and hunt with his neighbours, to care for his tenants and for the land on which they lived, to live himself as his fathers had before him and as his sons should do after him. They cannot have been happy years those which covered the time of his return home. His brother, whom he loved, had died six years before; his mother and father died within a year of each other. He was still unmarried, and his sisters were living when, in 1838, at the age of thirty-five, he succeeded to Hamsterley.

Characteristically his first action was to start a pack of hounds. His own note on the subject, "I got hounds," is the only record we have of their foundation; and two years later, in 1840, he gave them up without making mention of any reason for it. It may be that his approaching marriage left him less time for sport or that his new duties as squire made too many demands on him. It is said, with what truth it is now impossible to determine, that the hounds were a poor lot and were put down after some complaints of sheep-worrying. But in any case, if for only two years, he was again a master of hounds.

He entered seriously upon the new duties of his life, and in 1842 he was appointed a Justice of the Peace and Deputy Lieutenant for Durham County. Miss Moira O'Neill, writing in *Blackwood's Magazine*, June 1924, says, "Surtees was an exceedingly active and painstaking Justice of the Peace. It was his practice to take copies of notes of the cases that came before the Bench and these he never destroyed. Such notes were written on sheets of thin blue paper, 10 in. by 8 in., and he used the same stationery for his literary work." Above all he displayed an interest in, and knowledge of, the land and of agriculture. There is a long unpublished monograph of his written about this time which is generally known by the name Mr. Cuming bestowed on it, the "Description of Durham," which shows an awareness of the agricultural needs and problems of the day and he was especially keen on land drainage and fertilization. The only duties in which he apparently took no interest at all were those of a major in the Durham Militia, to which rank he was appointed in 1844. Considering his perpetual jeering at all soldiers, regular and irregular—the Heavysteed Dragoons, Lord Lavender's Yeomanry, Billy Bobbinson's troop and the like—it is little to be wondered at that he confessed "I never wore a sword." Not long after his gazette an official enquiry was made to him as to whether he would be willing to serve in the event of his unit being ordered abroad, and he promptly resigned. There seems to have been little chance of the

Mr. Jorrocks has a Bye Day

regiment going overseas then or at any other time, and it was probably little more than a courteous enquiry as to whether he proposed to give any attention to his military duties or not. He did not, and his resignation was a sufficient answer. We may be thankful for it. As we shall see in the Jorrocks Trilogy he was always inclined to make Mr. Jorrocks follow the incidents of his own life, often too closely for probability. Mr. Jorrocks as a country squire and an expert on land drainage and " nitrates o' sober " is preposterous enough. But at least we are spared Major Jorrocks riding Arterxerxes at the head of his squadron of the Duke of Donkeyton's Yeomanry or the Hillingdon Hussars. No doubt James Pigg would have been squadron sergeant-major, and Benjamin a trumpeter. On the whole it is as well that Major Surtees neglected his duties.

Though he had given up editing and returned to Hamsterley he still kept his taste for touring the country as a hunting correspondent. He could afford to take his own time over it now, to do it at his own expense and to choose which packs he visited. He was concentrating now on the science of hunting rather than on describing runs with various packs. He was well read in the hunting literature of his day, especially Peter Beckford, Smith, Vyner and Cook ; and the series of articles which he contributed to *Bell's Life* during the winter of 1845 to 1846, the best hunting winter in his recollection up to date, were intended to continue and develop their work. They were published in book form by Ackermann in 1846, with illustrations by Henry Alken, under the title *Analysis of the Hunting Field*. It is a book of limited interest to any except hunting men, and most of it deals with the duties, privileges and handicaps of various officials of a hunt, the master, huntsman, whipper-in and earth-stopper and of the groom. It is illuminated from time to time with flashes of his familiar humour and satire, particularly in the later chapters, where he deals with Lord Evergreen and tuft-hunting, Captain Shabbyhouse and horse-dealing, and Colonel Codshead. Yet in this work he is kindlier than usual to his dukes and earls for the sake of attacking the commoners who fawn on them. And he is even less kind than usual to women.

" Women," he writes, " are generally desperate tuft-hunters. There is no denying that. Many a poor man has been made to stoop to the scent who has no natural inclination that way. Tuft-hunting is an instinct that pervades nearly the whole sex. We have heard a tenth-rate milliner knock the peerage about with her tongue just as an expert billiard player knocks the balls about on the table." He makes play with the trite situation of a girl trying to secure a peer as a husband, which was to serve him *ad nauseam* in his novels, especially *Hillingdon Hall* and *Young Tom Hall*. It is poor, unworthy humour and he works it to death, but his attitude towards women is always one of the less pleasing things about him. It is some excuse for him that this type of human was the current coin of his contemporaries.

Nothing apparently delighted the Victorians more than the perfectly natural and sometimes pathetic phenomenon of an unmarried girl wanting a man. If in addition the girl were ageing or unattractive the jest was even more exquisite. W. S. Gilbert expended some of his crudest and most vicious fun on the subject, and the pages of *Punch* of those days are full of it. Surtees, though he differed from the Victorians in so many ways, adopted this convention. Probably he was so little interested in women and knew so little about them that it saved him trouble to use the popular form of humour, but it is hardly to his credit either as a man or as a writer. The subject is developed at wearisome length in *Young Tom Hall, his Heartbreaks and Horses*, in the pursuit by Angelena Blunt of Cornet Jug, Tom Hall and Lord Heartycheer. It is a type of humour now happily dead and not likely to be revived. We can well do without Katisha and Lady Jane, and without Angelena Blunt and Emma Flather, and the designing ladies of the *Analysis of the Hunting Field*. We prefer Surtees' other women—Lucy Glitters, who was always more pursued than pursuing, and even Mrs. Jorrocks, who for all her false ringlets and gooseberry eyes was capable of holding her own and of making her husband wish that his 'at covered his family.

Surtees himself married on 10th May 1841. His bride was Miss Elizabeth Jane Fenwick, daughter of Mr. Addison, J.P., of Field House, Co. Durham and Pallion Hall. His marriage and his political candidature at Gateshead are the two outstanding events of this period of his life, the period during which he succeeded to Hamsterley and during the whole of which he was busy with the Jorrocks Trilogy.

He stood as a candidate for Gateshead in 1837, and it is hardly necessary to say that he stood as a Conservative. He entered the contest under rather odd circumstances, as the Liberal Party in Gateshead had already put up a second Liberal candidate to oppose the sitting Liberal member, Mr. Cuthbert Rippon. Mr. Rippon was unpopular with a large number of the Gateshead Liberals on account of the irregularity of his private life, a subject about which Liberals are notoriously sensitive. Mr. Rippon was determined to seek re-election and his party put up against him a Mr. Williamson, less to uphold Liberal principles than to get rid of Mr. Rippon at any cost. The Conservatives saw in this splitting of the Liberal vote a prospect of regaining the seat and invited Surtees to contest it in their interest. He was quite willing, but learned at the outset that many Conservatives had already promised their votes to Mr. Williamson at a time when it seemed that no candidate would be forthcoming from their own party. Under the circumstances Surtees hesitated to complicate the issue any further and made a sensible and friendly proposition to Mr. Williamson.

"I find," he wrote, "that a portion of the electors of Gateshead are still desirous of recording their votes in favour of a candidate of their own politics and most likely will not promise you as long as a chance remains of that opportunity being afforded them. To remove this difficulty I have a proposition to make which I hope will meet your and others' approbation. Several gentlemen have promised you their votes under the impression that no other candidate of their Conservative opinions would present himself, and they will remain true to their promises in spite of their politics. My remaining in the field, therefore, will only have the effect of producing uncertainty and of returning Mr. Rippon should we go to a poll. I will at once then withdraw my address if you will agree, in the event of Mr. R's retiring, to release all your promises, and let us have a friendly struggle on political principles. . . . I should observe that in coming forward I was actuated by no unfriendly feeling towards yourself. The information I received in the South inclined me to believe that you were coming forward more to oblige the electors than from any desire of obtaining the seat: and, wishing to see the representation of the borough kept among the gentry of the district, I was induced to place myself in competition with one whose claims on the electors, I admit, are much greater than mine." He adds a P.S., "If a third candidate on the Whig or Radical side appears, this letter must not be considered binding."

It was a fair offer, but Mr. Williamson did not see his way to accept it. Mr. Rippon was determined to hold on to his seat if at all possible, and a three-cornered contest was inevitable. Surtees was late in the field, but he had high hopes from the splitting of the Liberal vote, and on the 10th of March he issued his address to the electors of Gateshead.

Gentlemen,

Since I first addressed you, another Candidate has appeared upon Principles so similar to those entertained by Mr. Rippon, as to afford you no choice on Political grounds. I am therefore induced, in Compliance with the earnest Solicitations of many of the Electors, to remain in the Field, which I should have left had Mr. Williamson's Opinions been such as Moderate Reformers can support. I will briefly state the Ground on which I seek your suffrages:

I am a decided friend to Improvement in every shape and way —a Reformer of proved Abuses in Church and State—an Advocate for the fullest Measure of Civil and Religious Liberty that is compatible with the Security of Property and the Maintenance of a National Religion: for Retrenchment and Economy in every Department of the Public Service—for the Extension of Commerce the Reduction of Taxation, particularly of those that press heavily on the Working Population and for the Diffusion of Useful Knowledge throughout the country. As a friend to the Church, I would support such a Measure of Reform as will provide for the improved Discipline of the Establishment, the Abolition of Sinecures, the apportioning of Emoluments to Duty, and the Prohibition of Pluralities, at the same time, I am desirous of relieving the Dissenters from Payments to which they entertain conscientious Objections, provided such Measure of Relief does not tend to compromise the Principle of a National Religion. I will not support any Measure either for this country or Ireland that appropriates any Portion of the Revenues of the Church to other than Religious Purposes, or that in any way weakens the Protestant Institutions of the Land. I have no objection to Triennial Parliaments, but am opposed to Ballot, unless the Votes of Members of Parliament be taken by Ballot also.

The Franchise I consider sufficiently low to place it within the Reach of all Men of Prudence and Industry, to whom its Attainment is an object of Ambition.

In conclusion, I beg to state that I will immediately resume my Canvass, when I shall be most happy to afford every Elector such further Information as may be required relative to my Political Creed: and in the meantime.

I have the honour to subscribe myself,

Gentlemen,

Your obedient and very humble Servant,

R. S. Surtees.

Hamsterley Hall, *March 10th,* 1837.

He made his position perfectly clear and it is true to say of him—as it is of few candidates—that he really was not anxious to be elected. He had come into the field at the desire of the Conservatives, who saw a chance of winning the seat owing to the dissension in the Liberal Party, but even at this late stage he was willing to withdraw if some way could be found out of the impasse. The main thing was somehow to unseat the undesirable Mr. Rippon, but the situation was not made easier by the fact that Mr. Williamson had up to the present time been a Conservative. His sudden conversion was caused mainly by the hope of securing the votes of those Liberals who were determined to get rid of Mr. Rippon, together with the votes of the Conservatives who, as no candidate from their own party was standing, would cast their votes for anyone who seemed likely to defeat him. The not unnatural result of this policy was that he irritated both sides, whereas Surtees, who stood openly as a Conservative and who had never been anything else, lost nothing in popularity by comparison with his opponents. It is indeed remarkable throughout the contest that, while the Liberal papers opposed his politics and principles, they spoke of him personally with nothing but respect—and that in days when personalities in election time were far more outspoken and less controlled than they are to-day. One Liberal paper observed that " the bold and frank demeanour of Mr. Surtees certainly deserved Radical approbation, and made that gentleman an object of respectful treatment." Another said that " it was evident Mr. Surtees had made a favourable impression," and a third, " we were pleased with his spirit and good temper and only regret that he is a Tory." And yet another summed him up as " an enlightened and Liberal Tory, whose address is a manly and creditable one, in which he declares his principles without the slightest equivocation." Their comments on their own alternative candidate, Mr. Williamson, were less flattering. " This shrinking from facing an opponent has evinced on his part a recreancy and cowardice of character that has sunk him many degrees below zero in public estimation. We should think that by his want of spirit he has rendered himself an object of contempt."

The occasion of this tirade was Mr. Williamson's refusal to attend a meeting called by the Mayor of Gateshead to consider the claims of the three candidates. Surtees had suggested that Mr. Williamson and he should both address the electors, who should then decide by show of hands which was the more suitable candidate to oppose Mr. Rippon. But Mr. Williamson was aware of the poor figure which he cut beside

Surtees and declined both that test and the alternative of the Mayor's Committee. So there was nothing for it but to put the three candidates to the test of voting. In those days voting was by show of hands, but any candidate who was dissatisfied with the result could demand a poll. On the show of hands Mr. Rippon was declared re-elected and a poll was demanded—by which of the other two is not recorded. Surtees saw clearly that either Mr. Williamson or he himself should stand down.

Mr. Williamson, difficult to the last, refused, so Surtees himself withdrew and left the rival Liberals to fight it out. The poll was held on 27th July, and by three o'clock in the afternoon Mr. Rippon was leading by so many votes that Mr. Williamson at last withdrew. Mr. Rippon retained his seat. Surtees had enjoyed a fight, earned good opinions in all quarters and gained some valuable experience which, as was his custom, he was shortly to bestow on Mr. Jorrocks in *Hillingdon Hall.* That he did make a good impression as a candidate is evident from the fact that during the next ten years he was repeatedly asked to stand again for various northern constituencies. It is equally evident that he did not want to be elected, because he steadily refused all invitations. Only once was he sorely tempted, and that in the following year, 1838, when Lord Londonderry wrote to ask whether he would be willing in the event of a vacancy occurring to contest the City of Durham. It was an important constituency and doubly interesting to him as having for so many years been represented by Mr. Ralph Lambton, the idol of his youth. But he had pledged himself again for Gateshead if anywhere, and at that time there were rumours that Mr. Rippon was about to apply for the Chiltern Hundreds. The rumours proved unfounded, the chance of Durham passed by and Surtees never offered himself for election again. But he always kept his interest in politics and he was a determined opponent of the Repeal of the Corn Laws. He always had the interests of his farming tenants at heart and he was convinced that repeal would mean ruin for the farmers of England.

The election in *Hillingdon Hall* is based on his experiences at Gateshead and on his feeling about the Corn Laws. As at Gateshead, there were three candidates in the field, two Whigs and a Corn-law Repealer, and, as at Gateshead, strenuous efforts were made to induce at least one of the candidates to withdraw. The official Whig candidate was the Marquis of Bray, heir of the Duke of Donkeyton, one of Surtees' typically amiable and imbecile aristocrats. He drew up his election address on the sound principle of saying as little as possible. The constituency had not been contested for many years, and the Donkeyton interest were staggered to find an opponent from the Anti-Corn Law League, Mr. William Bowker. Mr. Bowker first appears as Mr. Twister's clerk in *Handley Cross* in the office where Charlie Stobbs was articled, but, having fallen on evil days, he became a lecturer and traveller for the League. Mr. Smoothington, the Duke's lawyer, was directed to persuade him to withdraw and fortunately he proved more amenable than Mr. Williamson at Gateshead, for he accepted £1000 in cash and a rather nebulous promise of the Duke's interest in a distant constituency at a still more distant election. This seemed to leave the field clear for the Marquis, but unfortunately Mr. Smoothington had drawn up his address with such care to say nothing at all that he found himself labelled as an Anti-Corn Law candidate, especially as the League had written to ask him to avow his principles and he had not answered the letters. This so infuriated the farmers that they brought forward Mr. Jorrocks as alternative Whig candidate, but in support of the Corn Laws. Mr. Smoothington went into action again to try to induce Mr. Jorrocks to withdraw, but got nothing for his pains but a headache and a hangover. So Mr. Jorrocks and the Marquis went to the hustings, where Mr. Jorrocks distinguished himself with a speech that contains much of Surtees' own forthright manner, though probably Surtees did not deal with questions as cavalierly as did Mr. Jorrocks.

" 'Questins!' exclaimed our Squire, eyeing him with surprise. 'Questins!' 'I don't think,' added he, pulling out his watch and looking at it; 'I don't think I'm a-goin' to answer no questins.'

" 'Not answer any!' repeated the man with surprise.'

" 'No,' replied Mr. Jorrocks; adding, 'I've got a Mus*co*vey duck for dinner, and I'm afeard it'll be overdone.'

" 'Well,' observed the man in astonishment, 'I certainly shalln't vote for you!'

" 'P'raps you wouldn't ha' done that anyhow,' replied our Squire."

As at Gateshead, there was a show of hands and a poll was demanded, and Mr. Jorrocks was returned the winner by two votes. *Hillingdon Hall* closes—and with it the Jorrocks Trilogy—leaving Mr. Jorrocks a Member of Parliament.

During the present period of his life there are three incidents which cannot be ignored. Two of them nearly led to duels and the third might well have led to an action for libel. In the first case he was not a principal, and his conduct shows that, where he himself was not involved, he could display a tact and prudence which he would never have called to his own aid. He was asked to act as second in a duel by his old school friend Mr. John Hodgson Hinde, the Member for Newcastle. Mr. Hinde had quarrelled with a Major Orde, and the Major sent a challenge to him through a Colonel Younghusband. The challenge was of course sealed, and Surtees, who had no intention of letting his friend get involved in an unnecessary fight, did not break the seals. (They were actually first broken in 1923 by Mr. E. D. Cuming.) Mr. Cuming, who is the authority on this incident, says that " the cause of the quarrel is not quite clear, but it seems to have arisen from Major Orde's activity in promoting a petition against Mr. Hodgson Hinde's brother Richard, in the latter's election with Mr. Holmes for Berwick : Major Orde being the defeated candidate." " Surtees," he concludes, " evidently contrived to settle the business with Colonel Younghusband, for no reference to a duel can be discovered in those journals like the *Gentleman's Magazine*, which made a speciality of noticing ' meetings ' between gentlemen."

The second incident (in 1838), which has already been referred to, was the quarrel with Mr. J. W. Carleton, who wrote as " Craven " in the " Old " *Sporting Magazine*, in which he made some offensive remarks about Surtees. As Surtees himself was involved, there could be no question of adjustment or compromise and the only matter in doubt was whether Mr. Carleton was a gentleman and therefore a suitable opponent for Surtees. Surtees referred the question to his friend Mr. Grant the artist, who emphatically gave it as his opinion that a duel was out of the question. He quoted, as an example, Mr. Greville, who had also been insulted in print by Mr. Carleton about the running of one of his horses at Newmarket and who " never for a moment thought of fighting him, which if he had considered him as a gentleman he would of course have done." " It strikes me," Grant concludes sensibly, " this sets your question at rest. If Greville never could for a moment think of fighting him, I don't see how you can—unless it is an amusement which you particularly fancy."

And the last incident concerns Nimrod (Charles James Apperley) and marks the end of that desultory and unnecessary persecution of him in print which Surtees had carried out and to which reference has already been several times made. The last of these attacks was the Pomponius Ego incident in *Handley Cross* in 1843, where the portrait of Nimrod is as unkind as it is unmistakable. Nimrod, who was then living at Calais, saw a notice of the novel in the *Sunday Times* which commented on the obvious portrait of him and gently recommended

Surtees to curb his taste for personalities. Nimrod not unnaturally was hurt by this continued mocking, coming from a man with whom he hunted and whom he looked on as a friend, and wrote from Calais on 27th March :

SIR,

In a notice of your *Handley Cross* novel in the *Sunday Times* of yesterday, I find the following paragraph. "There is little of a personal nature in this entertaining production and that little is confined to a full length portrait of Nimrod, described as 'Pomponius Ego.' The picture though highly coloured is utterly unmistakeable." I feel myself called upon to demand on your part an *immediate* avowal or contradiction of this presumed fact.

Your obedient servant,

C. J. APPERLEY.

Surtees was not the man to disown anything that he had written nor to refuse a challenge from Nimrod. He replied at once :

SIR,

Yours of the 27th has just reached me here where I have been staying. In reply to your demand I beg to say the character of "Pomponius Ego" is meant for Nimrod.

Your obedient servant,

R. S. SURTEES.

But Nimrod had not yet read *Handley Cross*, and he answered sensibly and with restraint :

SIR,

I have received your letter avowing the fact imputed to you by the *Sunday Times*. Not having seen your book beyond the parts quoted in the *Quarterly Review* and the *Sunday Times* I am of course unable to say more on the subject until I have read the part relating to myself, which I shall take an early opportunity of doing and of addressing myself to you again.

Your obedient servant,

C. J. APPERLEY.

Even Surtees seemed to realize that he had gone too far this time and that it might be a good thing to get some advice. The offending passage in *Handley Cross* was quite enough to cause an action for libel, or even, since by any standards Apperley was a gentleman, a challenge. Surtees was never afraid of either, but in case either should threaten he would comply with the usual custom of putting himself in the hands of a friend. He selected Mr. Hodgson Hinde, for whom he had performed the same office six years before. Mr. Hinde was inclined to think lightly of the matter and wrote reassuringly :

> MY DEAR SURTEES,
>
> Most certainly I did not notice anything in your work, which I have read, personally offensive to Apperley . . . He has no right to find fault with your caricature of his egotistical style, nor with the giving his minute information of a day's sport of which he has seen little. I think it is probable you will hear no more from him, but if you do I shall be here till the day before Good Friday, when I go to Dover,
>
> Yours,
>
> J. HODGSON HINDE.

Mr. Hinde was right in saying that Surtees would hear no more of it, though not for the reason that he thought ; for within a few months Apperley was dead. He died at Calais in poverty and alone after a life of brilliance, extravagance and companionship. It is not pleasant to reflect that when Surtees launched this last attack he knew of the circumstances in which Apperley was spending his last days. He was a tenacious and bitter fighter, but this is one of the fights which must have given him little on which to look back with satisfaction. He tried to make amends with a memoir of Nimrod which was published as a foreword to Nimrod's *Life of John Mytton* in 1851. Yet in even this tribute there is something patronizing and acrimonious, as though the irritation which in life Nimrod had always aroused had not subsided eight years after his death.

"So lived and died," he wrote, "the celebrated popular Nimrod. We wish we could have reversed the order of his life and closed his days in the comfortable circumstances that attended his early career in the 'Old' *Sporting Magazine*. His great mistake was in quarrelling with that periodical." (In parenthesis it may be remarked that Surtees achieved the feat of quarelling not only with that periodical but with its successor the *New Sporting* and subsequently with the *New Monthly Magazine*.) He continues, " and the great mistake the proprietors of that work made was in allowing him to launch out too largely, and make his services too costly. There is no doubt that his contributions to the 'Old' *Sporting Magazine* had a very beneficial influence on its circulation, but he overestimated his capabilities and considered as permanent what in reality was only temporary. If he had been moderate in his ideas, a connection might have been formed that would have been mutually advantageous: for a sporting magazine was the true field for the development of Nimrod's peculiar talent.

" His forte was hounds, horses, hunting and driving, and on these subjects he was great. Whatever he wrote on other matters only tended to prove this. Nimrod had the honour of originating a style that died with him. We shall never see another Nimrod, another man taking the field as he did, received—we might almost say courted—by the great and affluent. Independently of the great expense necessary to equip such a character, it would be difficult to find another man sufficiently endowed with the attributes of a gentleman to undertake the office. This, however, we do not consider any loss. Hunting does not want the adventitious aid of art and never did. Nevertheless Nimrod was an acquisition in the times of limited locomotion in which he lived. He moved about, heard and knew all that was going on and had always an abundant stock of stories and anecdotes, which, being always told before fresh audiences, were quite as good as original ones. Nimrod was a great character, his name was known throughout the world, and his works will always be esteemed by sportsmen. He was a zealous and consistent advocate of hunting, and his writings have tended much to the comfort and advantage of that noble animal, the horse."

It is not the most gracious of tributes, but in some sense Surtees makes amends in it for the taunts of years. With Nimrod's death and this tribute the story of their association ends, and we can bid good-bye with some relief to a somewhat disagreeable episode.

Before we leave this period of Surtees' life it is necessary to notice if only briefly his very deep and real interest in the agriculture of his country. He succeeded to Hamsterley in 1838, and in 1861 he wrote an account of Durham farming. It only exists in the shape of a printer's proof with corrections in his own handwriting. " This essay," says Mr.

Cuming, "was obviously intended as a contribution to a work descriptive of the country, possibly of some larger enterprise: but assiduous search has failed to reveal its destination, and it seems probable that the topographical project met the fate of some other literary ventures and never saw the light." Mr. Cuming has given this paper the name of "Description of Durham," and it shows that during those twenty-three years Surtees had studied deeply and with sympathy the problems of the Durham agriculturist, especially of the small farmer. He had practical experience, for he farmed The Hagg of two hundred and fifty acres himself and managed some seven hundred acres of woodland. He used to keep a herd of from twenty to thirty beasts, steers, cows, calves and kyloes. "Kyloes" was the name for droving-cattle, and the great cattle-dealers used to drive thousands of these beasts southward every year to be fattened in Norfolk, Suffolk and Essex. The account books of Hamsterley show that the Surtees family were regular buyers of these cattle. The herds moved southward by the regular "cattle-ways," and the drovers had authority to sell any by the wayside if they found any farmers willing to buy. In *Hillingdon Hall* Mr. Jorrocks when out for a country walk meets "a large drove of Scotch kyloes, picking their way as they went. There might be fifty or sixty of them, duns, browns, mottles, reds, and blacks, with wildness depicted in the prominent eyes of their broad faces." (Incredibly the drover turns out to be James Pigg, Mr. Jorrocks's erstwhile huntsman at Handley Cross, arbitrarily transferred to *Hillingdon Hall* and losing as much in the process as his master and as Benjamin, his fellow servant.)

The "Description of Durham" contains a careful analysis of the difficulties that faced the small farmer in the district, shortage of capital uncertainty of leases and the Repeal of the Corn Laws being the principal. It deals too with the question of land drainage and land fertilization, which were pet hobbies of Surtees and by descent from him of Mr. Jorrocks. Indeed almost the only remaining trace in *Hillingdon Hall* of Mr. Jorrocks's early shrewdness is his invention of a draining-tile, the ingredients for which were to be obtained from his shop in St. Botolph's Lane. He also invented a preposterous machine which would perform practically every operation from sewing to threshing, but it never got as far as the stage of working-drawings. A more interesting part of the "Descriptions" deals with hunting and especially with Mr. Ralph Lambton, who was one of his earliest masters in the hunting field and with whom he continued to hunt whenever he could until the late eighteen-thirties, when Mr. Lambton was paralysed after a fall out hunting. It is pleasant reading, because it shows for once how Surtees could write in honest admiration of a man without trace of satire or depreciation. His final words about Mr. Lambton are very different from those that he wrote, for instance, about Nimrod.

" So lived and died the justly popular Ralph Lambton, an honour to human nature and a credit to the county to which he belonged. 'The evil that men do live after them, the good is oft interred with their bones,' says Shakespeare ; but so it has not been with him. His deeds were good and kind and just, and the name of the man and the fame of his hounds will flourish and expand as long as the County of Durham endures." Mr. Lambton's last accident in 1838 was the real reason for Surtees starting his own hounds at Hamsterley. For many years Mr. Lambton had made Hamsterley Hall his headquarters for the autumn and spring hunting, and Surtees started the pack to hunt that part of the country as soon as it was certain that Mr. Lambton would never be able to hunt again. A few years later, when Mr. Lambton was dead, the suggestion was made that Surtees should take over the whole of the Sedgefield Country that had been hunted by Mr. Lambton and hunt it himself with a subscription. To one who admired Mr. Lambton as he did it must have been a tremendously attractive invitation, but he was obliged to decline it. He was busy with his farming and was on the verge of marriage and had already given up his own hounds, so that it was impossible for him to spare the time which such an enterprise would need.

We may count the year 1845, the year of the publication of *Hillingdon Hall*, as the end of this period of his life. He was forty and now firmly established in his double life of country gentleman and sporting writer. He had succeeded to Hamsterley and to the duties of a Justice of the Peace and a Deputy Lieutenant. He had finished with journalism ; and besides dozens of papers on sporting subjects he had four published works to his credit—*The Horseman's Manual* and the Jorrocks Trilogy.

CHAPTER IV

Gone Away!

"Now where are all your sorrows, and your cares, ye gloomy souls! or where your pains and aches, ye complaining ones! one halloo has dispelled them all."—PETER BECKFORD.

"As soon as ever you 'ear the cry, make up your minds either to go on or go 'ome. But I won't s'pose that any man will stop stirrin' till the puddin's done."—*Handley Cross*.

I

"HANDLEY CROSS" was not a success and it was all Mr. Jorrocks's fault. Unlike Mr. Pickwick, he entirely failed to capture the public taste. His absorption with hunting made it probable that he would not have a very wide public; but it was the hunting public that he was put out to attract, and the hunting public refused to take him to their hearts. Had Surtees been as shrewd an observer of the trend of his times as he was of individuals, he might have hesitated at that juncture to make his cockney grocer a master of hounds. At just that time, as has already been noted, hunting itself was changing; and as the world became more democratic the hunt became more exclusive. The Corporation Hounds had come to an end; the tradesmen's packs were fast disappearing under the influence of the railways, which destroyed their country, and the growth of industrialism, which curtailed leisure, as England changed from an agricultural to an industrial country. The Jorrocks of the *Jaunts and Jollities* was in his element with the Old Surrey and the other London packs, but in *Handley Cross* he was an intruder into a world which was not his own. The tradition of the Midland and North and West Country packs, was one of aristocratic and gentle-born masters—Mr. Lambert, Lord Fitzwilliam, Mr. Hugo Meynell, Mr. Assheton and their like. Their followers looked with apprehension not unmixed with horror at the stout, be-wigged figure, mounted on his rat-tailed brown who ruled his hunt like any peer and imperiously told cavalry officers to "'Old 'ard, you 'airdresser." Typical of this class was Captain Freeman, Master of the

Southwold, and subsequently of the Old Berkeley, who scratched his head in bewilderment over the apparition. " What's the meaning of Jorrocks ? " he used to ask. " I don't understand that Jorrocks," he would say with a frown.

Mr. Colburn the publisher and Mr. Sholbert his literary adviser had seen the danger if Surtees had not and had even gone so far as to suggest cutting Mr. Jorrocks out of the book altogether—at least he should " prune down a little of the coarseness of the fox-hunting grocer."

But Surtees rarely took advice and in this case he was right in the long run if not at first. Yet " coarse " is the word which was used to describe Mr. Jorrocks at the time and for some years afterwards. Thomas Seccombe in the *Dictionary of National Biography* wrote, " The coarseness of the text was redeemed in 1854 by the brilliantly humorous illustrations of John Leech who utilized a sketch of a coachman, made in church, as his model of the ex-grocer. Without the original illustrations," he concludes loftily, " the works have very small interest."

Mr. W. P. Frith, R.A., in his *Life of John Leech* is even more scathing. " Amongst the many books illustrated by Leech," he wrote in 1881, " are some Sporting novels written, I think, by a Mr. Surtees. *Ask Mamma, Handley Cross, Plain or Ringlets, Mr. Romford's Hounds,* etc., owe their origin to this prolific gentleman. As these works are ornamented by coloured steel engravings and innumerable woodcuts by Leech, it has been my duty to look into them : read them I cannot. I hope if the author is still living he will attribute my want of appreciation to a want of sympathy with his heroes and heroines, though I admit in the portions that I have read that he shows considerable humour as well as power in expressing himself. This, from one who knows his own ignorance of the subject in question, should be gratifying to Mr. Surtees." Unhappily Mr. Surtees had died nearly twenty years before this graceful tribute was written so never experienced the gratification which he would undoubtedly have derived from the approval of the painter of " Derby Day." He would not have been gratified by Frith's remarks about Mr. Jorrocks. " He is M.F.H.," he wrote, " and so great an authority on sporting matters as to warrant his announcing himself as a lecturer on the duties of all concerned in the truly British sport of the chasing of the fox. Mr. Jorrocks's antecedents were such as to preclude the possibility of the display of brilliant oratorical powers. His mode of expression—including the absence of the letter 'h' where it should be used and its presence where it should not—was what might have been expected from the retired grocer whose little figure adorns the illustration . . . A curious reader can study Mr. Jorrocks's lecture in the pages of *Handley Cross*. He will there wonder with me how it came about that so distinguished an audience of aristocratic men, and lovely women, could listen for many minutes to an oration which must have lasted at least two hours, and which ends with the following peroration, 'So shall little Spooney jog on rejoicin'! Each succeedin' year shall find him better mounted, and at each fresh deal become a wiser, and, I 'opes, an 'appier man.'"

The Victorian age was nothing if not snobbish, as an age where wealth is the chief criterion must always be. "Coarse," is a word of various meanings, but as applied to Mr. Jorrocks it refers only to his antecedents and his ignoble trade of grocery, for the later Victorians had a horror of the class from which their own fathers came. Thackeray, who wrote in the old aristocratic tradition, and whose standard was always breeding rather than wealth, was far more sympathetic to the sporting grocer. He wrote in a letter to Surtees, "Mr. Jorrocks has long been a dear and intimate friend of mine. I stole from him years ago, having to describe a hunting scene with which I was quite unfamiliar, and I lived in Great Coram Street too." Thackeray was not a hunting man but he was an artist, and he recognized at once one of the great figures of English literature. He was also a gentleman and generous enough to be unsparing in his commendation of the work of a fellow author. Seccombe and Frith were—and quite rightly were—admirers of John Leech, and some men can only express admiration of an artist by damning his competitor or collaborator. Thackeray was not only an admirer but a personal friend of Leech, with whom he had been at Charterhouse, and it was he who suggested Leech to Surtees as the illustrator of *Mr. Sponge's Sporting Tour*. Surtees had wanted Thackeray to illustrate it himself, but Thackeray declined on the ground that he could not draw horses. "My friend Leech," he wrote, "I should think would be your man—he is of a sporting turn and to my mind draws a horse excellently. . . . You would find my pictures anything but comical, and I have not the slightest idea how to draw a horse, a dog or a sporting scene of any sort." He was equally generous in his appreciation of *Mr. Sponge's Sporting Tour* when it came out in 1853, and wrote :

SIR,

This is not to thank you for the grouse: but for the 2 last numbers of Soapey Sponge, they are capital, the Flat Hats delightful: those fellows in spectacles divine, and Scamperdale's character perfectly odious and admirable. I am come down hither in search of strength and fresh air.

Ever yours truly, dear Surtees,

W. M. THACKERAY.

The letter is dated from Brighton, is embellished with a pen-and-ink drawing of Lord Scamperdale and ends with the postscript, "If I've forgot your Xtian name don't quarrel with me." But Thackeray was almost alone among the Victorian novelists in his appreciation of Mr. Jorrocks. The general opinion was more nearly that expressed by Mr. J. G. Lockhart about *Nicholas Nickleby*—"All very well—but damned low."

Mr. Seccombe says that the text was "redeemed" in 1854 by the illustrations of John Leech, but the success of that edition was really due to the fact that it immediately succeeded the publication, in 1853, of *Mr. Sponge's Sporting Tour*, the first of Surtees' books which really caught the public fancy and the first which Leech illustrated. The first appearance of *Handley Cross* in the *New Sporting Magazine* was not illustrated nor was the first three-volume edition published in 1843 by Henry Colburn. Wildrake and Henry Heath illustrated *Hillingdon Hall* when it ran in the *New Sporting* from 1843 to 1844, and the three-volume edition in 1845 was not illustrated. *Hawbuck Grange* came out without illustrations in *Bell's Life in London* in 1846 and 1847, and the one-volume edition published in 1847 by Longman, Brown, Green and Longman had uncoloured plates by Phiz.

The association between Surtees and Leech began in 1852 with the publication of *Mr. Sponge* and survived through *Ask Mamma* and *Plain or Ringlets* to *Mr. Facey Romford's Hounds*, though Surtees had died the year before its publication in one volume and Leech only survived to complete fourteen of the proposed twenty-four illustrations, the remaining ten being provided by Hablot K. Browne. It is idle to speculate whether Surtees owed more to Leech, or Leech to Surtees. It was one of those rare combinations of two artists working hand in hand which produce such triumphs as the Savoy operas. Leech started with a tremendous advantage over most other illustrators of sporting novels in that he himself was a hunting man and understood horses. He had practically no drawing teaching at Charterhouse or afterwards, but he was intended by his father for the medical profession, and the thorough grounding in anatomy which he got at St. Bartholomew's Hospital was of life-long value to him. And he must have been a delightful person to work with. Even Surtees never quarrelled with him, though sometimes pressure of work made him late with his illustrations for the monthly parts in which the novels were issued. Leech was a man of singularly gentle and retiring temper and was quite content to be the junior partner in the joint concern. Even in matters of hunting and horsemanship, where he was quite at home, he deferred to Surtees, writing to him : " If anything in the way of *detail* presents itself to you that I might very likely leave out with my imperfect hunting knowledge, I shall feel greatly obliged by you putting me up to it. It won't do to make any glaring blunders." He was always anxious to realize the author's ideals and often wrote to Surtees to get his approval before introducing any idea of his own. When *Mr. Sponge* was in preparation Surtees showed that he too could be accommodating, writing to Leech, " If it will not discompose your arrangements, I propose making the editress of the Swillingford paper (the lady who makes such a hash of the hunt) a Bloomer."

It was quite the normal thing in such a partnership for the author to dictate to the illustrator, and Surtees was less peremptory in his demands that some of his contemporaries. When Hablot K. Browne was illustrating *Dombey and Son*, Dickens wrote to him : " *Subject*—These young men out walking, very dismally and formally (observe it's a very expensive school). I think Dr. Blimber a little removed from the rest, should bring up the rear or lead the van with Paul. I extract the description of the Doctor. Paul as last described but a twelve month older. No collar or neckerchief for him of course. I would make the next youngest boy about three or four years older than he." He then fell foul of Browne because he had put seventeen boys in the picture whereas Dickens had expressly stated that there were only ten.

The Victorian book illustrator was allowed little licence. His duty was to draw exactly what the author was describing and not to express his own ideas or personality.

The faithfulness in detail of those illustrators was astonishing. Every action, every furnishing, almost every hair on a head and fold in a dress that is mentioned in the text is to be found in the accompanying drawing.

It was not so much a time when artists illustrated books as when book illustrators were a class of artists who did that and little else and in consequence it was an age of great illustrators—Phiz, John Leech, Henry Alken and Du Maurier the pre-Raphaelites, and Aubrey Beardsley.

Surtees seldom describes the countryside. It may be, as Mr. Frederick Dawson suggests, that " the English landscape was sacred in a sense which his reticence shrank from turning into currency " or it may be that he was not particularly interested in it except as a background for his characters. At any rate his lack of concern with it gave Leech a free hand and in all the novels which he illustrated there are exquisite landscape backgrounds of the English countryside in sunshine and under rain and wind. Trees, grass, fences and woods are carefully and lovingly drawn ; and while the composition of all the pictures emphasizes the chief character, the backgrounds are never either perfunctory or conventional. In *Ask Mamma* there is an incident where Lord Ladythorne and Miss de Glancy are caught in a thunderstorm which spoils her beauty and quenches his ardour, and which is a repetition of the incident in *Young Tom Hall* with Lord Heartycheer and Angelena Blunt. It is a cruel type of humour, but Leech's illustration of the incident in *Ask Mamma* with its lowering sky and driving rain, its sodden ground and storm-tossed tree and above all with the grace of the girl's limbs thrown into relief by her sodden skirt is a thing of real beauty. Mr. G. D. Armour's drawing of the incident in *Young Tom Hall* leaves out the loveliness of the countryside and lays stress on the cruel bedragglement of Angelena. In many such ways Leech softens down the harshness of Surtees' humour and, in setting the main figures against a living countryside, makes them less targets for cruel wit than sharers in natural misfortune. Even Mr. Jorrocks, riding through the rainstorm on the World turned Upside Down Day or floundering in a mud hole near Pinch-me-near Forest, awakens more sympathy than derision. Surtees saw the humiliation of the situation and the impending colds, aches and pains. Leech drew a human being worsted by the tremendous power of nature.

II

Surtees was not the only fox-hunting novelist who was writing at that time, but on his own subject he was unquestionably the best, if not the most successful. He owed much of that lack of success to his attitude towards the sport—an attitude which he determinedly took up and stoutly maintained. Fox-hunting, as we have already observed, was changing as England itself was changing. It was becoming exclusive and aristocratic as the ancient régime closed their ranks to present an unbroken front against the advancing hosts of democracy. Its high priest was Charles James Apperley, and his leading disciple was Whyte-Melville. For Whyte-Melville as a writer Surtees had a great regard, and he recommended him to the newly published paper *The Field* as a sporting correspondent. Surtees himself had suggested the new venture of *The Field* and when he was asked to suggest a correspondent he wrote: "Whyte-Melville is out and out the best man of the day, being a very fine sportsman and a capital writer living in the very cream of the thing. Next to him Mr. Vyner would be useful or Mr. Horlock."

Surtees' suggestion of Mr. Horlock cannot be described as anything less than handsome, for Horlock disliked him and disapproved of his attitude towards the sport. W. H. Horlock, himself a master of fox-hounds, wrote in 1858 a book called *The Master of Hounds* in the preface to which and under the name of "Scrutator" he published an attack on the type of hunting novel represented by the recently published *Mr. Sponge's Sporting Tour*.

> My Dear Lord [he begins]
>
> By the following tale, in which the characters are depicted from real life, I have endeavoured to shew that Fox-hunters are not men of one idea only, or of one pursuit, and that Masters of Fox hounds do not, as they have been grossly misrepresented, *live for Fox-hunting alone*. As an exemplification of the contrary being the fact, I could adduce numerous instances, but need go no further than to point to your Lordship, now occupying the first position in the hunting world, as Master of the Quorn Country, and may affirm without flattery that the encomium bestowed on your great predecessor the celebrated Hugo Meynell, may with equal truth be applied to yourself—"He was, indeed, as much the *répandu* of the *élite* of Grosvenor Square—as much at home at St. James'—as he was at Quorndon or at Ashby pastures."

The allusion to masters who live for fox-hunting alone is of course to the Earl of Scamperdale in *Mr. Sponge*, and much fulsome and repellent flattery follows to convince Scrutator's noble patron that he is far removed from such a detestable character. That Surtees should recommend

Caught in the rain

[ASK MAMMA]

a man who could write such servile nonsense as a correspondent to *The Field* argues better for his kindness of heart than for his literary judgment. Horlock was of the school of Nimrod, to whom hunting was an affair of fast gallops, big jumps and sporting peers. Whyte-Melville too was a man of the " Shires," the son of an M.F.H. and himself an accomplished horseman. His novels are competent and often thrilling when hounds are running, but like Nimrod he saw everything in a haze of aristocratic romance. To both of them hunting was almost a sacred thing, the quintessence of noble England and the apotheosis of the Squire and the Earl.

There is nothing in them as there is in Surtees of the dirt and sweat of the chase, the smell of the stables, the dreariness of the hack home in the rainy evening. Charles Kingsley, a better writer than any of them, loved every minute of the hunt and was responsive to the appeal of wind and weather—so much so that his language describing the cry of hounds is almost that of lyric poetry. " Music ? " he wrote in *My Winter Garden*, " Well-beloved soul of Hullah, would that thou wert here this day and not in St. Martin's Hall, to hear that chorus as it pours round the fir-stems, rings against the roof above, scatters up into a hundred echoes, till the air is live with sound ! You love madrigals and whatever Weekes or Willyes or Orlando Gibbons sang of old. So do I. Theirs is music fit for men."

Anthony Trollope—who had hunted ever since he could afford to keep a horse—is similarly affected in *Orley Farm*. " And then the music of the dogs became fast and frequent, as they drove the brute across and along from one part of the large wood to another. Sure there is no sound like it for filling a man's heart with an eager desire to be at work. What may be the trumpet in battle I do not know, but I can imagine it has the same effect. . . . ' He's away ! ' shouted a whip from a corner of the wood. The good-natured beast, though as yet it was hardly past Christmas-time, had consented to bless at once so many anxious sportsmen and had left the back of the covert with the full pack at his heels."

" There is no gate that way, Miss Trustram," said a gentleman.

" There's a double ditch and bank that will do as well," said she.

One wonders what Mr. Facey Romford, who said that women were always getting in the way in the hunting field, would have thought of that. Mr. Jorrocks on hearing the " thief o' the world " described as the " good-natured beast " would surely have given vent to his favourite grunt of " Ookey Valker ! "

But how Mr. Jorrocks and Lord Scamperdale would have loved the M.F.H. in John Mills's *The Old Hall*, published in 1847! Like Lord Scamperdale, he couldn't curse or use foul language, but, unlike Lord Scamperdale, he had no Jack Spraggon to do it for him. "I must beg of you," said the Squire, riding up to the side of the offender, "to be quiet. It is far from my wish to say anything that might offend or wound the feelings of the humblest individual who joins my hounds, but I will not permit unsportsmanlike conduct . . . Learn to be quiet, Sir, learn to be quiet, and you'll set the best example that heads the rules for gentlemen to observe in the field." One can only hope that so temperate a rebuke brought tears to the offender's eyes and that it proved as effective as Mr. Jorrocks's "'Old 'ard, you 'airdresser!" and Mr. Spraggon's "Oh you scandalous, hypocritical, rusty-booted, numb-handed, son of a puffing corn-cutter, why don't you turn your attention to feeding hens, cultivating cabbages, or making pantaloons for small folk instead of killing hounds in this wholesale way?"

John Mills is unknown to-day, but in his time he too threw his little brickbat at Surtees. In 1868—three years after the publication of *Facey Romford*—he wrote in *British Sports and Pastimes,* "The books that we have had about hunting men have too frequently described to us a set of loud ignorant men, who are always halloaing 'Yoicks' and who are generally exercising the keenest of their intellects in cheating each other out of a ten-pound note in some matter of horseflesh. We remonstrate most loudly against this representation of the hunting field."

The whole hunting world—or at any rate that part of it which was erudite enough to write a book—seems to have remonstrated most loudly against Surtees. Even one of Surtees' old school friends joins the ranks, for Robert Ingham, Q.C., who had been at Ovingham with him, wrote: "There is one defect I should like to hint at. Why not make your satire effective by restraint? Do give us a good character, man or woman; honest, truthful, domestic, trying to do what duty requires to God and Man, and happy accordingly. You are only in your first number [of a serial] and you could easily weave one golden thread in your fabric."

It was an intensely moral age. Trollope in his *Autobiography* expresses the creed of the Victorian novelist.

"The novelist," he writes, "if he have a conscience, must preach his sermons with the same purpose as the clergyman, and must have his own system of ethics. If he can do this efficiently, if he can make virtue alluring and vice ugly, while he charms his readers, instead of wearying them, then I think Mr. Carlyle need not call him distressed nor talk of that long ear of fiction, nor question whether he be or not the most foolish of existing mortals.

"I think that many have done so, so many that we English novelists may boast as a class that such has been the general result of our own work . . . Coming down to my times, I find such to have been the teaching of Thackeray, of Dickens and George Eliot. Speaking as I shall speak to anyone who may read these words with that absence of self-personality which the dead may claim, I will boast that such has been the result of my own writing. Can anyone by search through the works of the [six] great English novelists I have named find a scene, a passage or a word that would teach a girl to be immodest or a man to be dishonest?"

Trollope was an honest man and no humbug and an extremely competent writer of fiction. He must be credited with having written this in good faith, and it represented fairly the attitude and belief of all his contemporaries. It is little wonder that they looked askance at the world of Surtees with its imbecile aristocrats, dishonest horse-dealers, sporting grocers and swindling masters of hounds. For Surtees annoyed them all equally. He was quite aware of the opposition and of the feeling that he aroused. His old friend Ingham told him of it, Captain Freeman, the Master of the Southwold, added his puzzled endorsement. And in *Hawbuck Grange* Surtees himself carried the fight to his opponents and took the words out of their mouths.

"What queer books you write!" observed our excellent but rather matter-of-fact friend Sylvanus Bluff, the other day, who seeing us doubling up a sheet of paper in a rather unceremonious way, concluded that we were at what he calls our "old tricks." "I buy all your books," added he with a solemn shake of the head, as though we were beggaring him—"I bought your *Jorrocks's Jaunts and Jollities.* I bought *Handley Cross, or the Spa Hunt,* I bought *Hillingdon Hall, or the Cockney Squire:* but I don't *understand* them, I don't see the *wit* of them. I don't see the *use* of them. *I* wonder you don't write something useful."

The publication of *Ask Mamma* raised something of a storm against the moral character of Mrs. Pringle; and Mr. Frederick Dawson records Surtees' remark that his wife considered her "a far more respectable lady than Lucy Glitters." So the echoes of the chorus of criticism were heard at Hamsterley and Mrs. Surtees put in her word in her husband's defence.

But he needed no defence. He had never feared opposition, and as it gathered and grew after the publication of the Jorrocks Trilogy his satire became more biting, his blows were dealt out more widely and more fiercely. The publication of these books covers a period of fourteen years—from 1851 to 1865. The humour never fails, the satire never weakens. Surtees did not mellow with advancing years, but he developed technically as his satire became more keen-edged and his humour less kindly. He did not oblige his old friend Mr. Ingham by weaving one golden thread into his fabric, unless one can reckon the single figure of Mr. Jovey Jessop in *Plain or Ringlets*. He did not emulate Trollope in making virtue alluring and vice ugly, because there is no virtue in his books in Trollope's sense and the only instance of the punishment of vice is the failure of Mr. Sponge's cigar-shop. He was not interested in virtue or vice, only in hounds, men and horses. He preached no sermon, though in the preface to *Mr. Sponge* he went so far as to warn ingenuous youth against dishonest horse-dealers. He was neither a tuft-hunter, a moralist nor a sentimentalist, and he was not to be turned from his course by the protests of any of those classes of society. What he became after *Handley Cross* and remained to the end was a satirist. And during those fourteen years between 1851 and 1865 he wrote five novels which for sustained interest, technical achievement and sheer humour are unmatched in the record of English satirical literature.

III

There is no doubt that Surtees' claim to immortality depends very largely on the Jorrocks of *Handley Cross*. He stands with Falstaff and Sir Toby Belch, Mr. Pickwick and Mr. Micawber, in the gallery of the great comic characters in English Literature

The truly great comic character is rare—much more rare than the hero or the tragic figure. He is rare because he is the most difficult person of all to create. Unless he is to deteriorate into a butt, a mere figure of fun, he must possess characteristics other than humour. He must be, as Falstaff was, " not only witty in himself but a cause of wit in others " —a cause of wit, be it noted, not a target for it. He must possess a definite character of his own with attributes which are lovable and even admirable and he must be to a certain extent in control of events and not entirely at their mercy. He may love food and wine, but not be a glutton or a drunkard, suffer mischances, but never be quite overcome by them, indulge his fancy and his wit but never lose touch with reality. He must in fact, unless he is to degenerate into the pure buffoon, have the natural dignity which comes from being a genuine and complete person. Above all he must be aware of his own weaknesses, able to laugh at them, but on occasion able to conquer them. And perhaps even most important he must be ready of speech, quick at repartee and easily quotable.

Given these qualities—and it is a formidable list—he may do almost anything, because he will be able to extract humour from anything. And there are certain qualities which are shared by almost all the great English characters. They are nearly all on the wrong side of the law at one time or another in their lives : they nearly all display a prodigious thirst and often an equally prodigious hunger : they are always hard up : and—somewhat surprisingly—they often feel and show a spice of timidity even of cowardice.

The last is a surprising taste in a nation that has always exalted physical courage to a place above all the Christian virtues. Mr. Jorrocks once said that " there was no young man wot would not rather have a himputation on his morality than on his 'ossmanship." There are probably few Englishmen who would not own to any failing rather than physical cowardice : so that a man will fail again and again in justice, in mercy and in chastity and yet hold his head high, while a momentary failure of nerve will be a lifelong reproach to him. Yet in fiction and in drama the comic hero's timidity never fails to bring a round of applause. Falstaff feigns death when faced with the Percy : Sir Andrew Aguecheek declines the invitation to the duel with Viola : Bob Acres feels his courage oozing out at the palms of his hands : and Mr. Jorrocks never goes off the 'ard road if he can 'elp it. There is in us all a spice of cowardice, actual or potential, though we conceal it as well as we can from others and from ourselves. A fictional character who feels this emotion, admits it and can make a jest of it is very near to our hearts. In the same way the hunger and thirst of the comic hero touch a chord in most of us. There are probably more jokes about drink in English humour than about any other subject except matrimony.

It may seem strange that dignity should be claimed as an attribute of a comic character, but unless he has it he cannot be a great one.

" Now," Mr. Jorrocks says in one of his sporting lectors, " let ingenuous youth suppose himself at the meet and that he has been presented to the M.F.H. to whom the greatest respect and reverence should always be paid, for there's no man to compare with him ' i' point o' greatness.'" "Of all the sitivations under the sun," he says on another occasion, "none is more enviable or more 'onerable than that of a master of fox'ounds ! Talk of an M.P. ! vot's an M.P. compared to an M.F.H. ? You M.P. live in a tainted hatmosphere among other M.P.s and loses his consequence by the commonness of the office, and the scoldings he gets from those who sent him there, but an M.F.H. holds his levee in the stable, his levee in the kennel and his levee in the 'untin' field—is great and important everywhere—has no one to compete with him, no one to find fault, but all join in doing honour to him to whom honour is so greatly due." His consciousness of his office comes out in the awful dignity of his official letters written in the third person—a trap for the uneducated, as Mrs. Jorrocks found, but one which he evades with success and with a portentousness which would not have disgraced the Duke of Wellington. Sir Archibald Depecarde of Pluckwelle Park had a vicious horse which he wanted to dispose of and he thought—not knowing Mr. Jorrocks—that he would be a suitable buyer, so he invited him over to Pluckwelle Park to see it. "M.F.H. John Jorrocks," Mr. Jorrocks replied, "presents his compliments to Sir Archibald Depecarde and in reply to his favour begs to say that he will take an early hopportunity of driving over to Pluckwelle Park to look at his quadruped and as the M.F.H. 'ears it is a goodish distance from Handley Cross he will bring his night cap with him, for where the M.F.H. dines he sleeps and where the M.F.H. sleeps he breakfasts." On another occasion a Mrs. Martha Lucas appeals to him to subscribe to redeem her mangle and he answers "M.F.H. John Jorrocks presents his compliments to Mrs. Martha Lucas and is sorry to hear of the sitivation of her patent mangle : but the M.F.H. having laid it down as a rule never to subscribe to redeem patent mangles cannot depart from it in her case." Seldom can a subscription have been refused in such high-sounding words even if we cannot help feeling that he might have departed from his rule in this case—after all his own mother had been a washerwoman.

But the dignity conferred by an office is worthless unless that office is honourably upheld and its duties appreciated as well as its privileges. It could not be said that the office of Master of Hounds conferred much dignity on, for instance, that drunken rascal Sir Harry Scattercash who was "just enough of a master of hounds to be jealous of the neighbouring ones." But Mr. Jorrocks was well aware of his responsibilities. He makes his position perfectly clear in his first oration at Handley Cross.

"You see, I've comes down to 'unt your country, to be master of your 'ounds in fact—and first of all I'll explain to you what I means by the word master. Some people call a man master of 'ounds wot sticks an 'orn in his saddle and blows when he likes, but leaves everything else to the 'untsmen. That's not the sort of master of 'ounds I mean to be. Others call a man a master of 'ounds wot puts in the paper Mr. So-and-so's 'ounds meet on Monday at the Loin o' Lamb: on Wednesday at the Brisket o' Weal: and on Saturday at the Frying-Pan: and after that, jest goes out or not, as suits his convenience—but *that's* not the sort of master o' 'ounds *I* means to be . . . In short I means to be an M.F.H. in reality and not in name . . ." Mr. Jorrocks was as good as his word: he was a M.F.H. in reality and not in name. His meets were regularly advertised, he was always punctual at the covert-side (even if after the night before he felt as if he'd "eat a straw 'at or a pair o' worsted stockin's.") He knew and cared for his hounds and he kept discipline among his hunt servants—no light task when the servants were James Pigg and Benjamin. He had a thorough control over the financial side of the hunt and paid due regard to its social side. In fact he knew his job and did it to the best of his considerable ability.

In the field he rode hard, though he never jumped if he could help it. He was afraid of it, but that he did jump when he had to is obvious from the frequent entries in his journal: "paid for catching my 'oss 6d," "paid for catching my 'oss 2/6d." The whole record of his mastership of the Handley Cross is a proof of his possession of that dignity which comes from the true fulfilling of an important office.

But he had to the full too that other, truer sort, the dignity which comes from being an entire and genuine person. There was nothing sham or pretentious about him, and he hated sham and pretentiousness. He was a self-made man, but without the usual failings of that class. "Mr. Jorrocks was a great city grocer of the old school, one who was neither ashamed of his trade, nor of carrying it on in a dingy warehouse that would shock the managers of the fine mahogany-countered, gilt-canistered, puffing, poet-keeping establishments of modern times. . . . As a merchant he stood high—country traders took his tea without tasting, and his bills were as good as bank notes. He was 'highly respectable' as they say on change—that is to say he was very rich, the result of prudence and economy—not that he was stingy, but his income outstripped his expenses and money like snow rolls up amazing fast."

His extraction was obscure and the very little that we know of his early days we glean from the *Jaunts and Jollities* and from *Hillingdon Hall*. His mother was a washerwoman, but she must have died when he was a little boy, for he was brought up in Camberwell by his grandmother. The only other fact that we know about his family is that he had a brother Joe with whom he quarrelled over the division of a buttered muffin—a quarrel that was to be lifelong and indirectly to lead to his own marriage. The future Mrs. Jorrocks's parents encouraged the courtship and hastened on the marriage for fear that he might become reconciled to Joe and leave his fortune to his nephews. So he must have married fairly late in life if by that time he had acquired a fortune and Joe a family. But that is all we ever learnt about it.

Most self-made men fall into one or other of two errors—they either try to conceal their origin or else they boast about it. Mr. Jorrocks did neither. He hated humbug and pretentiousness, and it comes out most strongly during his visit to Cockolorum Hall. Mr. Marmaduke Muleygrubs, J.P., the owner, was another self-made man, but a very different type from Mr. Jorrocks. " Mr. Marmaduke Muleygrubs had been a great stay-maker on Ludgate Hill, and in addition to his own earnings (by no means inconsiderable) had inherited a large fortune from a great dry-salting uncle in Bermondsey. On getting this he cut the shop, bought Cockolorum Hall, and having been a rampant Radical in the City was rewarded by a J.P.-ship in the country." Mr. Jorrocks knew all about Mr. Muleygrubs and was not impressed by this new splendour. The picture gallery full of ancestors was dismissed as " such a lot of stay-makers," the best state bedroom as " a fine tuppeny 'ead and farthing tail," the footmen as " three o' those powdered poopies," while the dinner itself, which was long, elaborate and very bad, elicited the audible comment, " God bless us ! what a dinner ! " The difference between the two men, the genuine and the bogus is clear in their conversation from the moment of Mr. Jorrocks's arrival at Cockolorum Hall.

IV

Nearly all the great comic heroes are good trenchermen and Mr. Jorrocks was no exception to the rule save that, being (unlike most of them) a very rich man, he was never short of the means of appeasing his appetite and his thirst. Throughout this trilogy and indeed throughout the Surtees novels there is a rich and unashamed delight in food and drink. It may be that it compensated Surtees for the bread-and-milk breakfast of Ovingham and the dreary meals of the London coffee-houses, though he himself was personally abstemious all his life. He used to write at Hamsterley, standing at a reading-desk propped on a table, and his wife used to have to summon him to meals or, when the work was going exceptionally well, to bring his dinner in to him. But he understood food and wine, and the details of the meals in his novels are meticulous and full. It was a time of great eating and drinking. To the starved stomachs and pinched palates of these austerity-stricken days the menus sound gargantuan, though it must be remembered that Surtees' contemporaries only had two main meals a day, breakfast and dinner, and that they rode and walked a good deal more than we do to-day. Mr. Jorrocks took his breakfast very early and his dinner at " five o'clock and no waiting " and he spent nearly all the hours in between in the saddle, hunting or exercising.

In the *Jaunts and Jollities* he gave a dinner for eight people (one of whom was Mr. H'Apperley Nimrod) at which the fare consisted of two tureens of mock-turtle soup, each capable of holding a gallon and brim full : turbot and lobster sauce and a great salmon : boiled beef and an immense piece of roast, six brace of grouse, basted calf's head, leg of mutton, chickens, ducks, plum puddings, tarts, jellies, pies and puffs. But he never judged a menu by its length. He was a master grocer and he knew quality when he saw it. The pretentious but unsatisfying menu of Mr. Muleygrubs' dinner aroused his outspoken contempt. He audibly calculated its cost as the meal proceeded. " Humph ! not much there—three shillins' for the top dish, one for the bottom and eighteen pence, say, for the four sides, five and six altogether —think I could do it for five." But when Mr. Jorrocks was not entertaining and had only himself to please his menus are a marvel of brevity and succulence. When he went to stay at Pluckwelle Park and the resources of Sir Archy Depecarde's larder were thrown open to him he selected a " couple o' dozen hoisters, cod and hoister sauce, a beef steak and a fizzant." He disdained sweets, " didn't care nothing 'bout soup 'less it was turtle," and " filled up the chinks wi' cheese." And some of his other dinners are noted in his journal, often accompanied by a lament that the chances and delays of the hunting field will cause him to be late and the dinner to be spoiled. " I wish I was well back at the Cross, with my 'ounds safe i' the kennel—Vot a go this is ! Dinner at five—baked haddocks, prime piece of fore chine, Portingal honions and fried plum-puddin'."

" Oh dear ! Oh dear ! " he moans after another mischance " shall never see my dinner this day, Torbay soles with Bude cockle sauce, Dartmoor Forest mutton, puddin' and taters under the meat." It is consoling to remember that though he never got his dinner on either of these two occasions, on both of them he found a good substitute. On the former he dined at Ongar Castle and in the latter he fell in with a smuggler and was hospitably entertained to pig's fry, jugged hare, oatcake and cheese, bottled ale and illicit whisky—incidentally the only time in the three books when Mr. Jorrocks is mentioned as drinking whisky.

But once he could not eat the " best dinner wot ever was cooked —turtle soup and turbot—haunch o' doe wenison and Stilton." It was the day on which he read Pomponius Ego's account of the Handley Cross Hounds which so upset him that he lost his appetite. " Couldn't eat a bit," he sadly records—and when Mr. Jorrocks couldn't eat his dinner the world was out of joint indeed.

He was—as a comic hero should be—a good trencherman but no glutton, and in a deep-drinking age he drank deeply but he was not a sot. His favourite drinks were port and brandy and water, which he took either " 'ot with " or " cold without." His taste in port was the same as Mr. Sponge's. He liked " a strong military wine," one " that leaves a mark on the side o' the glass " and " gets a grip on the gob." His normal consumption after dinner was not less than one and not more than two bottles to his own cheek, which compares favourably with Mr. John Mytton's average, as given by Nimrod in his " Life," of not less than four bottles a day, the first drunk while he was shaving in the morning. After the dinner at Pluckwelle Park he remarked " I had just as good a drink as a man can wish for. A'most two bottles of undeniable black strap, besides et ceteras, and no more 'eadache than the crop o' my w'ip." The et ceteras had included a bottle of champagne, which he had refused to have put on ice on the grounds that " I doesn't want to 'ave all my teeth set a chatterin' i' my 'ead : hain't got so advanced in gentility as to like my wine froze—I'm a Post Office Directory, not a Peerage, man."

When he was entertaining he was as lavish with drink as he was with food. Pomponius Ego after dining with him wrote in the article in the " Heavy Triumirate," " But my readers will naturally inquire 'Had you, Ego, with all this eating, anything like drinking in proportion ?' 'Oh, indeed I answer yes—Oceans of Port ! We drank

Fox-hunting again and again and again. In short, whenever my inestimable host found himself at a loss for a joke, a toast or a sentiment, he invariably exclaimed, " Come, Mr. Ego, let's drink Fox-'unting again ! " Particulars I will not enter into, but I may be allowed to speak for myself. I paid such devotion to Bacchus that I fancied I became the God myself!'"

With such meals and such oceans of port it is no wonder that Mr. Jorrocks attained that fullness of figure which distinguished so many comic heroes—Falstaff, for much the same reason, walks before his page " like a sow that hath o'erwhelmed all her litter but one," though when he is out of sorts he complains that " my skin hangs about me like an old lady's loose gown. I am withered like an old apple-john." We are never allowed to know what Mr. Jorrocks weighed, because he would never get into the scales to see whether he was " nearer eighteen stun or twenty." " He didn't ride stipple chases," he very wisely said, " and wot matter did it make 'ow much he weighed ? It was altogether 'twixt him and his 'oss, and weighin' wouldn't make him any lighter." But, having to be at the expense of mounting him, he made a point of enquiring James Pigg's weight before he engaged him. " Ar's long but ar's leet," replied Pigg, looking down at his spindle shanks, " Ar's sure a dinna ken what a weighs—maybe eleven stun."

Every comic hero must have his foil. James Pigg the hard-riding, hard-drinking, north-country huntsman is the perfect foil for Mr. Jorrocks. They were united by a common love for hunting and for brandy and water. It was this latter taste that gave rise to that most famous piece of dialogue when the night was hellish dark and smelt of cheese, and later to the agreement which they entered into that one or other of them should always remain sober the night before hunting. About most other things they differed sometimes violently—the most resounding of their clashes was on the " Cat and Custard-Pot " day when Mr. Jorrocks took the desperate step of discharging Pigg and hunting the hounds himself. It was not one of his happiest experiments and might have ended disastrously had not the discharged Pigg turned up unexpectedly, taken hold of the hounds, killed the fox and restored himself to his master's favour. But Pigg is much too important and complete a character to be nothing but a stooge for Mr. Jorrocks. Next to Jorrocks he dominates the book, and Surtees wisely recognizes his worth by allotting to him a fair share of scenes by himself without Mr. Jorrocks to stand in his light. Pigg, too, except in keenness, is the antithesis of his master in the hunting field. He rode hard and shirked nothing and, as a good huntsman should be, he was always up with his hounds. Where Mr. Jorrocks was often in at the death by a judicious process of gate-opening, short-cutting and road-riding, Pigg went straight over fence and water. He is a strange, uncouth figure with his outlandish northern accent, his cousin Deavilboger and his " brandy and baccy'll gar a man live for iver." He occupies in *Handley Cross* very much the position that Sam Weller does in the *Pickwick Papers*, that of a secondary figure but one of enough humour and importance to support a good share of the work on his own shoulders. From a purely artistic point of view Surtees' handling of Jorrocks and Pigg is one of his finest achievements. They are complimentary to each other, and yet apart from each other they are equally good. The balance is better than in the *Pickwick Papers*, where Sam Weller is inclined to put his master in the shade when they appear in company, but that is probably less because Weller outshines Pigg than because Mr. Jorrocks outshines Mr. Pickwick. The actual keeping of the proportion between Mr. Jorrocks and Pigg is a marvel of novelist's tact, and Pigg is compensated by being allowed to tower above Benjamin and Batsay, the other two supporting figures of the Jorrocks household. They all reappear in *Hillingdon Hall,* Pigg somewhat improbably as a cattle drover, Benjamin quite impossibly as clerk to the Justice of the Peace, but they do not bear transplanting. And it is significant of the change from one book to the other that we hear no word in *Hillingdon Hall* of the enforced marriage between Pigg and Batsay which was foreshadowed at the end of *Handley Cross*.

V

The comparison between Mr. Jorrocks and Sir John Falstaff is inescapable. " Jorrocks," says Mr. Frederick Dawson " was vulgar, as Falstaff was vulgar. Both were noisy, intemperate, boastful and self-confident. But both were English in flesh and bone and if Jorrocks was vulgar he was not hypocritical. His secret lies in his sincerity." And Professor Bonamy Dobrée gets even nearer to the true comparison when he says " Jorrocks is without doubt an imaginative creation : he is of the race of immortal and divine fat men. In a sense he is the Falstaff of the chase : for he is something of a fairy with a superb gift of variegated invective and an unanswerable repartee."

Surtees knew his Shakespeare, and there are quotations from the *Henry IV* plays in several of the novels. It is almost impossible to think that he had not Falstaff in his mind when he was creating Jorrocks. True there are great differences. Falstaff was a gentleman by birth if seldom by behaviour, Jorrocks was the son of a washerwoman. Falstaff was a rogue, Jorrocks was an honest man. But they shared an enormous relish for life, a readiness for all its chances and an ability to cope with its pitfalls. They shared a rich delight in food and drink, in jest and repartee and in the society of their fellow men. They shared too that particular type of timidity which is so endearing in the comic hero.

Mr. Jorrocks did himself less than justice when he told Mrs. Muleygrubs that he was the hardest rider in England, because he " never went off the 'ard road if 'e could 'elp it." He was never afraid of the pace as long as there was no leaping and he would jump a fence if he could not find a gate or a gap or get James Pigg to punch a hole in the fence before he went over it. " Terrible nasty place," he soliloquizes once when Arterxerxes has landed him safely over an open ditch, " should ha' been drund for a certainty if I'd got in. Wouldn't ride at it again for nothing under knighthood." Mr. Jorrocks's one intention was to kill his fox and to be in at the death if he could manage it. Surtees was a capable and fearless horseman ; Jorrocks was a shrewd and careful one. Neither was a thruster and both of them hated and despised thrusters. It was a feeling that underlay so much of Surtees' feeling about Nimrod, the feeling that is so evident in the difference between Hotspur's rant,

> " By heaven methinks it were an easy leap,
> To pluck bright honour from the pale-fac'd moon."

and Falstaff's cynical " What is in that word honour ? Air. A trim reckoning ! Who hath it ? He that died o' Wednesday." To Jorrocks and to Falstaff honour is a shadow and they were men of substance.

Professor Dobrée speaks of " a superb gift of variegated invective and an unanswerable repartee." There is no more essential part of a comic hero's equipment and Falstaff and Jorrocks shared it to an extraordinary degree. Whatever difficulties Falstaff involved himself in he never failed to extricate himself with a timely jest, an adroit turning of the tables, but it is never a mere verbal score. Prince Hal's repartees to Falstaff are wittier and more cruel than Falstaff's to him. Falstaff's verbal triumphs—and they are frequent and colossal—are not so much victories of words as the welling-up of an immense personality that dwarfs all his opponents with its humour and its humanity. Prince Hal could score off Falstaff in words, but he could never make him look or feel small.

Mr. Jorrocks and Pigg drink " Fox-Hunting "

[HANDLEY CROSS]

Falstaff's humour, as Jorrocks's, is the humour of the common man not the polished shaft of the drawing-room. It is the function of the comic hero to deliver the repartee that we ourselves should have delivered had we thought of it in time or had the courage to let it fly.

In just such a way did Mr. Jorrocks demolish the bewhiskered officer of the Ninety-First.

" ''Old 'ard !' roars he to the forward roadsters, who were now getting among the hounds, 'You 'airdresser on the chestnut 'oss !'—holloaing to a gentleman with very big ginger whiskers—'Pray 'old 'ard !'

" 'Hairdresser !' exclaims the gentleman, in a fury, turning short round ; 'I'm an officer in the ninety-first regiment !'

" 'Then you hossifer in the ninety-fust regiment, wot looks like an 'airdresser, 'old 'ard,' replied Mr. Jorrocks, trotting on."

He was ready with a repartee on the most inauspicious of occasions. On the dreadful Pomponius Ego day, when Pigg was surly and Benjamin impudent, when Xerxes and Arterxerxes had been recklessly treated with ginger by Pigg so that their tails stuck up like hat-pegs and when finally Arterxerxes kicked Mr. Jorrocks off over his head, a certain Mr. Gillyflower, whom he hated, expressed the hope that he was not hurt.

" 'Hurt !' exclaimed Mr. Jorrocks, his eyes sparkling with rage as he scrambled up and replaced his lost head-gear, 'hurt, sir,' he repeated, looking as though he would eat him, 'no, sir—not at all—rather the contrary !' "

But he met his match in James Pigg on the " Cat and Custard-Pot " day when Pigg was too drunk to hunt the hounds and Mr. Jorrocks set about him.

" 'There are as good fish i' the sea as ever came out on't !' replied Mr. Jorrocks, brandishing his big whip furiously ; adding, 'I'll see ye leadin' an old ooman's lap-dog 'bout in a string afore *you* shall 'unt' em.'

" 'No, ye won't !' responded Pigg. 'No, ye won't ! Arve ne carle te de nothin' o' the sort ! Arve ne carle te de nothin' o' the sort ! Arle gan back to mar coosin Deavilboger's.'

" 'You may gan to the devil himself,' retorted Mr. Jorrocks, vehemently—'you may gan to the devil himself—I'll see ye sellin' small coals from a donkey-cart out of a quart pot afore you shall stay wi' me.'

" 'Thou's a varra, feulish, noisy, gobby, insufficient 'ard man !'

retorted Pigg, 'and ar doesn't regard thee! No; AR DOESN'T REGARD THEE!' roared he, with a defiant flourish of his fist.

"'You're a hignorant, hawdacious, rebellious rascal, and I'll see ye frightenin' rats from a barn wi' the bagpipes at a 'alfpenny a day and findin' yoursel', afore I'll 'ave anything more to say to ye,' rejoined Mr. Jorrocks, gathering up his big whip as if for the fray.

"'Sink, arle tak' and welt thee like an ard shoe, if thou gives me any mair o' thy gob,' rejoined the now furious Pigg, ejecting his baccy and motioning as if about to dismount."

Honours, we may say, are even. Falstaff-like, Mr. Jorrocks had said his say and Falstaff-like, when blows threatened, he mounted his horse and rode away. But good as Mr. Jorrocks's repartee was it was not his sole verbal resource. There is barely a page in *Handley Cross* when he does not say something shrewd, humorous, memorable. There is good talk of almost every sort—pithy reflections like "There must be unanimity and concord, or we shalln't kill no foxes," and "Con-found all presents wot eats." Full-dress orations like the Sporting Lectors and the speech at the Handley Cross Hunt dinner. Lyrical outbursts that approach the realms of poetry when hounds are running: "Oh, beautiful, beautiful! Oh, beautiful indeed! 'Ow true to line! Best 'ounds in England by far—never were such a pack!" And the pæan of praise that begins, "How I wish I was a heagle!" Rich torrents of vituperation mostly addressed to Benjamin: "Oh, you epitome of a tailor! You're of no more use with 'ounds than a lady's maid—do believe I could make as good a whipper-in out a carrot! Get off, ye useless apology of a hosier and pull it down or I'll give you such a wopping as'll send you to Blair Atholl for the rest of the day." To a hound: "Rot ye! ye great lumbering henterprizeless brute! Rot ye! d'ye think I boards and lodges and pay tax 'pon you to 'ave ye settin' up your 'olesale himperance that way? g-e-e-t away, ye disgraceful sleepin' partner of the chase!" And, of course, to Arterxerxes: "Dash the beggar, but I wish to was a-top on 'im, I'd give 'im summat to run for. Dash my vig! But I'd give ye summat to run for if I had 'old on ye—I'd make ye cry capevi, my friend!" There are, too, his more sombre moods of dignity and despair.

Of dignity: "'Who be those?' enquired Mr. Jorrocks with great importance.

"'Captain Smith and Lieutenant Brown,' replied the soldier-groom, saluting.

" 'Foot-captins, I presume?' replied our Master, looking at their horses.

" 'Grenadier Company,' replied the man.

" 'It's all the same to me,' replied Mr. Jorrocks. 'They didn't expect I'm again to 'unt sich a day as this—do they?' "

And of despair:

" Oh, dear! Oh, dear! was there ever sich an misfortunit individual as John Jorrocks! was there ever an independent British grocer made sich a football on by fortin? Tossed about the world like an old 'at. Tempted from the 'olesomest, the plisantest, the most salubrisome street i' London to take these 'ounds, and then be drawn into this unpardonable wilderness. Nothin' but rushes and grass that Nebuchadnezzar 'imself would turn up 'is nose at!"

And finally his reflective mood when he contemplates his own death:

" I once wrote my epitaph and it was werry short—

'Hic jacet Jorrocks'

was all wot I said: but the unlettered 'untsman, or maybe M.F.H., might pass me by, jest as 'e would a dead emperor. Far different would it be should this note follow: 'Mr. J. was a celebrated fox-'unter and lectorer upon 'unting!' Then would the saunterin' sportsman pause as 'e passed and drop a tribute to the memory of one who loved the chase so well."

But there is no end to it, one could go on quoting for ever. Falstaff himself was no richer in wit and words, Sam Weller no quicker in repartee. Mr. Jorrocks's speech varies from grave to gay, from vituperative to ecstatic, from sardonic to genial. There is line after line, page after page of it, and yet it never palls because it is always varying. He was a master not only of hounds but of the spoken word. He was in fact a celebrated fox-'unter and lectorer upon fox-'unting. We may leave it at that. It was his own epitaph.

CHAPTER V

Check

"Ha ! a check. Now for a moment's patience ! We press too close upon the hounds ! . . . We shall now see if they will hunt as well as run." —Peter Beckford.

"'Old 'Ard !" repeated he, holding up his hand. "Appallin' sound !" added he mournfully, "fearful to the forrard and dispiritin' to all. Now's the time when the M.F.H., if he has any mischief in him and 'appens to be hup, will assuredly let drive at some one."—*Handley Cross.*

I

The vagaries of the English climate had seldom been more in evidence than in the years 1845 and 1846. During those twenty-four months they ran their full gamut through every season. The summer of 1845 was as wet and cold as only an English summer can be. But it ended at last, and in compensation there followed one of the finest autumns and most open winters within the memory of any then living. "But when they *did* begin hunting," Surtees writes, "what a season they had ! Almost a surfeit—to the short stud ones, certainly a surfeit. We have not had such an early season since Plenipo's year." November brought the "glorious, sloppy, burning-scent sort of weather peculiar to that month. November is generally the freshest, greenest spot on memory's hunting waste." Throughout that winter there was hardly a day when hunting was not possible, and the season lingered long in the memories of hunting men. It was perpetuated in Surtees' "Analysis of the Hunting Field," which appeared in *Bell's Life in London* from October 1845 to April 1846 and was published in one volume by Ackermann later in the same year.

The year 1846 was as treacherous as its predecessor. Winter slipped almost imperceptibly into spring to be followed by a summer of roasting heat and another winter, one of frost, snow and tempest. "The November of 1846," Surtees writes in *Hawbuck Grange*, "to which season the following adventures of our friend Mr. Scott are confined, was the worst hunting season perhaps ever known. It was more like a bad

March . . . a nasty, harsh, windy, mutton-broth, cold-in-the-head, shivering-shaking sort of affair. The fact is that the year 1846 was a month in advance of itself all the way through and we had November in October." It was no new thing for the months to become confused in their weather, as Titania knew.

As the *Analysis of the Hunting Field* perpetuates 1845, so *Hawbuck Grange* does the same for 1846. But the vilest winter, like the worst summer, ends at last and 1847 came in. It was a memorable year for Surtees. *Hawbuck Grange* ran under the name of "Sporting Sketches" in *Bell's Life*, from October 1846 to June 1847, and was then revised and published in one volume by Longman, Brown, Green and Longman. And in this year, six years after his marriage, his first son was born. He was christened—as were all the eldest sons of that branch of the family—Anthony. As it proved he was the last Anthony Surtees to inherit Hamsterley, for he never married, and died in Rome in 1871. The estate passed to his elder sister, Miss Elizabeth Surtees, who died, unmarried, at Brighton in 1916 (where her father had died in 1864), and on her death, to her sister Miss Eleanor who had married the fifth Viscount Gort. The two sons of that marriage were Field-Marshal Viscount Gort, V.C., who commanded the British Expeditionary Force in France in 1939 and 1940, and the Hon. Standish Robert Gage Prendergast Vereker, M.C., the present owner and occupier of Hamsterley Hall. Mr. Vereker married a Surtees—Miss Bessy Surtees of Dinsdale, another branch of the family that flourished at Hamsterley, Dinsdale, Mainsforth and in other places in Northumberland and Durham.

During the last hundred years the men of the Hamsterley Surtees have not been long lived. Since 1810, three Anthonys and one Robert died, and in 1871 the name of Surtees of Hamsterley became extinct.

II

The original name under which *Hawbuck Grange* appeared in *Bell's Life*, and in a somewhat different form, was "Sporting Sketches," and even in its final one-volume form it is more like a collection of sketches than a complete novel. It is the most loosely constructed of all Surtees works, and is really little more than a number of isolated incidents, more or less bound together by the presence at all of them of the pleasant but uninteresting Tom Scott. It would be a great improvement to the book if Chapters XIII to XV were cut out altogether as they have no bearing on the story, and are unworthy of their author. Chapter XIII is devoted to the wholly ridiculous and unnecessary incident of the meet at Fast-and-Loose Castle, with the reincarnation of Surtees' old Brighton friend Baron Gablenz, and the incredible performance of Billy Bobbinson's Yeomanry—a performance which can only be explained by the fact that Surtees' undistinguished military career in the Durham Militia had ended abruptly not long before the book was written. Chapter XIV consists of a childish hoax played by Tom Scott and Gurney Sadlad on Joe Tugtail, to describe which five lines of print would have sufficed and even then have been wasted. And Chapter XV leaves Tom Scott to look after himself, and becomes so confused a meteorological report of various hunting years, that the reader is left in some doubt and even more indifference as to what the weather really was like in the ten years between 1837 and 1847. And in any case the essential information has already been given quite adequately in Chapter I, and repeated for good measure in Chapter III. Chapter XVI (the last) returns to the story of Tom Scott, but the interest has gone out of it and the last few pages are surely some of the most slipshod and perfunctory that Surtees ever wrote.

Hawbuck Grange seems to have been conceived as a sort of comic compendium to the *Analysis* and then hastily and somewhat carelessly recast into the form of a one-volume novel. It is a sad piece of amateur carpentry, and the joints creak and gape in an alarming fashion. There is no plot at all, but this is hardly surprising as Surtees disliked plots and as far as he could avoided them. In the preface to the original edition of *Ask Mamma* in 1858, he wrote, "It may be a recommendation to the lover of light literature to be told that the following story does not involve the complication of a plot. It is a mere continuous narrative of an almost everyday exaggeration, interrupted with sporting scenes and excellent illustrations by Leech."

Hawbuck Grange had excellent illustrations not by Leech but by Phiz. It has plenty of sporting scenes and a good measure of exaggeration, but it has no narrative and it is certainly not continuous. It is like a cake composed of the finest and richest ingredients which the cook has forgotten to mix. There are plums in it in plenty and sugar with a spice of vinegar. But the dough is indigestible. And yet, its faults of construction apart, it is one of the most genial and most charming of all his books. The character of Tom Scott contributes much to this. He is no great comic figure, no Jorrocks or Sponge or Romford, but a decent, unpretentious and honest hunting farmer. Surtees writes in the preface, " Tom Scott, seeing his Adventures advertized as the sporting adventures of ' Thomas Scott Esquire,' wrote to us to say that he calls himself *Mister*—Mr. Thomas Scott and that he has ' Thomas Scott, Farmer, Hawbuck Grange ' in honest parliamentary-sized letters, without flourish or eye-mystifying gewgaw, on the back of his dog-cart, as anyone who likes to inspect it may see." He may have had " Farmer " printed on his cart, but that seems to have been the limit of his efforts in the farming line, for he spends his whole time in hunting. He shows the same lack of enthusiasm for his courtship, though he is contemplating marriage with a Miss Lydia Clifton and, though he once nearly goes as far as to ride over to see her on a non-hunting day, it is no surprise when she writes to him at the end of the book to tell him of her engagement to a cousin, Harry Crow. Tom makes some conventional complaints, but we cannot believe that they are heartfelt. Surtees apparently decided to have a normal human being for a hero for once, and so allowed him a love affair : but his constitutional lack of interest in women overcame him, and he only remembers Miss Clifton at the end and then summarily dismisses her. It is typical of Surtees that the honesty and love of opposition which were always in him should make him just at this juncture come out so strongly in favour of the currant-jelly men. But his attitude is perfectly logical. They had hunted the hare with Anthony Surtees' hounds at Hamsterley when he was young and he understood the sport as few fox-hunters did. He never fell into the error of regarding hare-hunting as an inferior copy of fox-hunting, for he knew it was a sport in its own right, as ancient and honourable as its more fashionable counterpart. He knew the skill and patience required to hunt a hare when the scent is weak or grows cold and to his mind, which was always absorbed with the science of hunting rather than riding, it was as great a skill as was required to hunt a fox over the wide grasslands of the Midlands.

His whole case was that the hunting should be careful, thorough and appropriate to the country, and that it should be within the capacity of the men, the hounds and the horses. He is always especially severe on the hunts like Sir Harry Scattercash's, who followed the fox because it was the thing to do though neither the resources nor the men of the hunt were capable of it. " Fox-hunting should be done handsomely ! " he writes in *Hawbuck Grange*. " There is something about the noble animal that forbids one treating him slightingly. He should be hunted like a gentleman. What chance have a lot of trencher-fed, milk-fattened, street-scouring beggars with a good, high-couraged clean-feeding, well-conditioned flyer ? None whatever. . . . Nothing can be more pitiable than the half-rigged turn-out of an ill-supported pretension to a fox-hunt. The boosey-looking huntsman (generally the saddler or publican)—the wretched, broken-kneed, overworked, leg-weary job horse—the faded half-jockey, half-huntsman-looking caps, the seedy, misfitting, Holywell Street-looking coats—the unclean boots and filthy breeches—with the lamentable apologies for saddles and bridles. We never see a Tom-and-Jerry-looking 'scarlet' without thinking how much more respectable the wearer would look in black. We never see a country-scouring, fence-flattening field without thinking how much better they would be with a pack of harriers."

Surtees had a fine gift of vituperation, and when he is really roused he is always profuse in epithets, and particularly in hyphenated epithets. But there is no snobbery in this outburst ; rather is it an attack on the snobbery that must needs hunt the fox without the equipment to do it properly. To do it properly, that is the great thing with Surtees whether it be hare or fox. Pretentiousness was always the great sin in his eyes.

In *Hawbuck Grange* the prejudice in favour of hare-hunting is strong. The Goose and Dumpling Hunt are held up as an example of careful and serious devotion to the sport. " The hounds are as good as can be and have been in existence nearly forty years, during the whole of which time the greatest care and attention have been paid to their breeding. The members of the hunt are all sportsmen, men who love hunting innately, but who take no pleasure in leaping." It is Surtees' old creed : the hound rather than the horse, the hunt than the gallop, the gap or gate than the fence. It is the hunting of Anthony Surtees at Hamsterley.

There is nothing uncertain about the next book, *Mr. Sponge's Sporting Tour.* From the very beginning we are plunged into the underworld of hunting. As each character is introduced a few lines of description tell us without ambiguity what we are to expect. Mr. Sponge himself is " a good looking rather vulgar man. At the distance—say ten yards—his height, figure and carriage gave him somewhat of a commanding appearance, but this was rather marred by a jerky, twitchy, uneasy sort of air, that too plainly showed he was not the natural, or what the lower orders call the *real* gentleman." He " wanted to be a gentleman without knowing how." Mr. Benjamin Buckram, " though very far from being one, had the advantage of looking like a respectable man."

Mr. Leather, his head man, is " one of the fallen angels of servitude." Mr. Waffles, first of the wealthy young men on whom the " hangers-on " batten, is " a pretty man " in appearance and dress and incessant in conversation. " His tongue was never at fault. It was jabber-jabber : chatter, chatter : prattle, prattle, prattle : occasionally about something, oftener about nothing." Caingey Thornton, first of the " hangers-on," is " as big a little blackguard as any in the place—lives on Waffles, and yet never has a good word to say for him, nor for no one else—and yet to 'ear the little devil a-talkin' to him, you'd really fancy he believed there wasn't not never sich another man i' the world as Waffles—not another sich rider—not another sich racket-player—not another sich pigeon shooter—not another sich fine chap altogether."

Not a character comes into the book without some such cynical introduction, and when Surtees comes to Sir Harry Scattercash and his " hangers-on " he fairly lets himself go. Sir Harry himself is " a tall, wan, pale young man, with a strong tendency to delirium tremens ; that, and consumption, appeared to be running a match for his person." And his friends : " They were all captains, or captains by courtesy. Ladofwax had been a painter and glazier in the Borough, where he made the acquaintance of Captain Quod, while that gentleman was an inmate of Captain Hudson's strong house. Captain Bouncey was the too well-known betting-office keeper."

Two of the principal characters of the book are Jack Spraggon, greatest of " hangers-on," and Facey Romford, whom we shall meet again in a later book. Mr. Romford is first introduced to our notice as a " great, round-faced, coarse-featured, prize-fighting sort of a fellow, who lived chiefly by his wits, which he exercised in all the legitimate lines of industry—poaching, betting, boxing, horse-dealing, cards, quoits—anything that came uppermost. . . . Having the apparently inexhaustible sum of a thousand pounds, he began life as a fox-hunter—in a very small way to be sure—more for the purpose of selling horses than anything else ; but having succeeded in ' doing ' all the do-able gentlemen, both with the ' Tip and Go,' and ' Cranerfield hounds,' his occupation was gone, it requiring an extended field—such as our friend Sponge roamed—to carry on cheating in horses for any length of time. Facey was soon blown, his name in connection with a horse being enough to prevent anyone looking at him."

Jack Spraggon was killed in the Grand Aristocratic Steeplechase, almost the only occasion in all his novels when Surtees essayed pathos.

The occasion might have been more successful had not Mr. Spraggon been a character whose passing it is impossible to regret. His epitaph is spoken by his patron, the Earl of Scamperdale, " Oh, my dear Jack ! Oh, what a treasure, what a trump he was ! Shall never get another. Nobody could slang a field as he did : no humbug 'bout him—never was such a fine natural blackguard."

In fact, seldom in any book has there been such a collection of fine, natural blackguards. And nearly all of them, of course, are engaged in the pursuit of horse-dealing. In the preface, Surtees suggests that his object in writing it is to warn " ingenuous youth " against such transactions. " The author," he writes, " will be glad if it serves to put the rising generation on their guard against specious, promiscuous acquaintance, and trains them on to the noble sport of hunting, to the exclusion of its mercenary, illegitimate off-shoots." Horse-dealing is Mr. Sponge's primary interest, and he hunts not " for love of the thing " but simply to show off the horses which he has to sell. In this pursuit he is seconded by Mr. Buckram, the dealer, and by Leather, Mr. Buckram's head man. Sponge never owns a horse himself. He hires them from Mr. Buckram with the object of selling them on a profit-sharing basis. To such a combination Mr. Waffles with his £100,000 in the " funds " is a godsend, and it is not long before he falls a victim to them in the affair of the brown horse Hercules.

Mr. Sponge's comment on the deal is " *Con-found* it ! I don't do myself justice. I'm too much of a gentleman. I should have had £500—such an ass as Waffles deserves to be done ! "

Mr. Sponge is the most consistent and successful horse-dealer in the book, but by no means the only one. Nearly everyone at one time or another is interested in buying or selling a horse from, to, or for a friend or acquaintance.

But it is not Mr. Sponge's only accomplishment. He has a perfect genius for imposing himself as a guest on his acquaintances. He goes from Jawleyford Court to Hanby House, from Hanby House to Puddingpote Bower and from Puddingpote Bower, with a brief and unsatisfactory interlude in Mr. Facey Romford's lodgings, to Nonsuch House. All his hosts begin by welcoming him and end by trying to starve him out ; but as a guest Mr. Sponge is as tenacious as he is unsolicited. The only man who is equal to him is Mr. Romford, who fed him on pork and sausages, played the flute to him and won money off him at *écarté*. True Mr. Romford never got paid ; but even to have got the better of Mr.

Sponge over a game of cards is more than anyone else in the book achieved.

The most disreputable and dissolute characters, in a book that is replete with them, are found at Nonsuch House where the drunken Sir Harry Scattercash presides over a mob of captains, real and sham, and actors; and it is at Nonsuch that we first meet Lucy Glitters, the most important feminine character in the Surtees novels, who eventually becomes Mrs. Sponge and reappears in *Mr. Facey Romford's Hounds*, where she keeps house for Mr. Romford and passes as his sister. In herself she is an uninteresting person, but as an amateur whip and horse-dealer she is of some value to both of her men. Her love affair with Mr. Sponge is as colourless and perfunctory—except that it ends in marriage—as that of Tom Scott and Lydia Clifton.

One point that is of special interest in *Mr. Sponge's Sporting Tour* is the importance which Surtees gives to descriptions of the clothes of his characters. It must have been partly the result of his collaboration with Leech, for Leech is constantly writing to him suggesting and making enquiries about the colour of the ladies' dresses and the men's evening coats. Surtees had always taken an interest in dress. His description of Mr. Jorrocks's costumes in the *Jaunts and Jollities* is detailed and meticulous. In *Sponge* he takes the trouble to describe the clothes worn by nearly every male character in the book. And as the distinction is clear in his mind between those who hunt for love of the thing and those who hunt for any other reason, so there is no mistaking the difference between the man who is properly dressed for hunting and the man who is not. There are nearly two pages of description of the hunting clothes in which Mr. Sponge, the workman, turns out—the double layer of cloth on the outside of the sleeves, the low-narrow-collared coat with the seams outside, the broad ridge and furrow of the white cord waistcoat, the heavy, close-napped hat and the mahogany tops. It is a smart turn-out, but everything in it is made and worn for use rather than show. To Surtees the hunting-man's dress is the outward sign of the seriousness and honesty of his hunting intentions. The Flat Hat Hunt was a serious pack, and Lord Scamperdale and Jack Spraggon dressed for work and not for show, though they were helped in this by the fact that their clothes and even their spectacles were interchangeable.

"There had been a great deal of rain in the night, and the horses poached and squashed as they went. Our sportsmen, however, were prepared as well for what had fallen as for what might come: for they

Jawleyford and his tenants

[MR. SPONGE'S SPORTING TOUR]

were encased in enormously thick boots, with baggy overalls and coats and waistcoats of the stoutest and most abundant order. They had each a sack of a mackintosh strapped on to their saddle-fronts." Lord Scamperdale and Jack were hunting the fox, as he should be hunted, like a gentleman, and so invariably was Mr. Sponge who was always "got up with uncommon care in the severe order of sporting costume." Very different was his host, Mr. Jawleyford of Jawleyford Court, whose costume consisted of a green-and-gold yeomanry forage cap, a tremendously stiff stock, a bright, green cut-away coat, velvet coloured and single-breasted, a blue waistcoat covered with horse-heads and a pair of rhubarb-coloured tweed pantaloons. But as Surtees observed, "Gentlemen unaccustomed to public hunting often make queer figures of themselves when they go out. We have seen them in all sorts of odd dresses—half fox-hunters half fishermen, half fox-hunters half sailors, with now and then a good sturdy cross of the farmer."

The matter of dress may seem unimportant, but it is clear that to Surtees it was far from it. It was one more evidence of the difference between the serious and the spurious hunting man which had always been so clear in his mind and which is the turning-point of all the remaining novels.

Mr. Sponge made his first public appearance in the *New Monthly Magazine* in January 1849 and continued regularly till April 1851. The editor of the *New Monthly* was Mr. William Harrison Ainsworth, who had succeeded to the position in 1845. By that time the magazine was already thirty-one years old and it was well established, with a high literary reputation. Among previous editors had been Bulwer Lytton, Tom Hood, Theodore Hook and Thomas Campbell. Ainsworth, the historical novelist, was a happy choice, for he was a man of wide reading and discriminating taste: moreover, he had inherited from his north-country, Dissenting ancestry a shrewd business head and an imperious temper which made him an efficient and decisive man of affairs. But he had, too, an ingenuous snobbery and a personal vanity which showed itself in his first advertisement and in his subsequent habit of publishing photographs of himself in all the magazines which he edited or controlled. In 1845, when he became editor of the *New Monthly Magazine*, he announced the fact and with it coupled an intimation that under his management the magazine would be supported by authors "eminent not only for talent but for high rank." This was too much for Thackeray, always on the look out for snobs, and he took

Mr. Sponge at Jawleyford Court

Ainsworth to task in *Punch*, which was then under the editorship of Mark Lemon, recently one of Surtees' colleagues on the *New Sporting*. Heading his article "Immense Opportunity," he wrote: "Mr. Ainsworth, on whom the Editorship of the *New Monthly Magazine* has 'devolved', provides a list of contributors to that brilliant periodical and says he has secured the aid of several writers 'eminent not only for talent BUT FOR HIGH RANK.' Are they of high rank as authors or only in the Red Book? Mr. Ainsworth can't mean that the readers of his magazine care for an author because he happens to be a Lord—a flunky might—but not a gentleman who has any more brains than a fool. A literary gentleman who respects his calling doesn't surely mean to propitiate the public by saying, 'I am going to write for you—and Lord Fitzdiddle is going to write too.'"

By a strange chance before the article appeared in *Punch* an invitation to contribute to the *New Monthly* had been despatched from Ainsworth to Thackeray, who accepted it in a friendly and characteristic letter in which he made it clear that he did not abandon the position which he had taken up. The two dined together and composed their difference, and thereafter Thackeray wrote regularly for the *New Monthly*. But *Punch* continued to poke fun at Ainsworth, especially at his innocent love of publishing his own portrait. In January 1849, in a column headed "Seasonable Benevolence," Mr. Punch remarked that "Mr. Harrison Ainsworth was about to publish another portrait of himself in one of his magazines when, seized with a sudden fit of seasonable benevolence towards his readers, he altered his mind." And later in the same year Mr. Punch promised that "The next book Mr. Harrison Ainsworth publishes will contain 'Four Portraits of the Author.'" But these harmless foibles apart, Ainsworth was a pleasant companion, and both Thackeray and Surtees were on friendly terms with him. Also, and more important, for all his taste for contributors of high rank he had a sound literary judgment and enough confidence in it not to be swayed by an author's previous lack of success. The Jorrocks Trilogy had not sold well, and *Hawbuck Grange* had sold very badly indeed. But Ainsworth, though no sportsman himself, wanted a sporting story for his magazine and recognized in Surtees the supreme sporting writer of the day. It was not a light decision to take to allot space in a monthly magazine for nearly two years ahead to an author who was not yet fully established, but he made it without hesitation and success justified it. Mr. Sponge proved to be a great attraction and held the public interest throughout his magazine career. Ainsworth was generous too in his encouragement, writing several times to Surtees in strong approbation of the story, and giving him practically *carte blanche* as to the length of time which he needed to run the book to an end. He showed the same generosity when in 1851 *Young Tom Hall, his Heartbreaks and Horses* succeeded *Mr. Sponge* in the *New Monthly*, writing to Surtees of the earlier chapters : " They are all that can be desired. Go on in the same vein and you cannot fail to please everybody." Later on in the year he wrote again to Surtees to ask how long *Tom Hall* was likely to continue, adding, " I only want an approximate idea, that I may arrange accordingly with other matters." Surtees estimated that he would need a further six months, to which Ainsworth replied : " Six months more of *Tom Hall* will just do and bring him to a pleasant and proper close. For though I individually could go on reading such a good story for ever and never tire I am afraid that the eternal craving after novelty might not be altogether of my opinion." There could hardly be a more friendly letter, yet it contains the first faint hint of one of the causes between them which was to destroy their friendship and interrupt *Tom Hall.* Surtees, of all men, had neither sympathy with the craze for modernity nor any idea of curtailing one of his works to oblige the cravers after it, or even to oblige Mr. Ainsworth.

But an editor, after all, must have some say in such a matter ; and with one as disposed to be friendly as was Ainsworth it is unlikely that this point alone would have caused a breach between them. There were other sides to the character of each of them which made one almost inevitable and which in fact caused the final rupture. To begin with, their views on the subject of advertisement were diametrically opposite. Ainsworth's taste was flamboyant and, as we have seen, he was not above making capital out of the name and social standing of his authors. He was anxious to use Surtees' name because it now carried some weight as the editor of the *New Sporting* and the author of several sporting novels, and also—Ainsworth's snobbish taste being quite irrepressible even by Thackeray—because he was a country squire and had been a master of foxhounds. But on this subject Surtees was adamant. " I find," he wrote to Ainsworth, " I can write much better and with far more pleasure to myself when I am free to deny authorship if I like." So in spite of Ainsworth's pleading both *Mr Sponge* and *Tom Hall* appeared in *New Monthly* as " by the Author of *Handley Cross.*" But Ainsworth was only biding his time, and in December 1851 when *Tom*

Hall had been running for about three months he inserted an advertisement mentioning Surtees by name. Whether he did it by accident or, as is more probable, by design has never been decided, but whichever it was it proved to be the spark that set off the inevitable explosion.

An explosion was inevitable because, for all their difference in upbringing and taste, there was something very much alike in the two men. They were both from the North Country, with their full share of their countrymen's obstinacy. Both of them had a high sense of their own dignity and were accustomed to having, and determined to have, their own way. Ainsworth, the successful author and proprietor of several magazines, Surtees, the Master of Hounds and Squire of Hamsterley, were in the habit of laying down the law and of being obeyed without question. The matter of the advertisement could have been composed between two men of more accommodating temperament. But neither of them would go an inch to meet the other, and an acrimonious correspondence put an end to a profitable association and to a personal friendship.

But this was not to happen till January 1852. From 1849 to 1851, while *Mr. Sponge* was running in the *New Monthly*, they were on the best possible terms. *Mr. Sponge* was proving successful; Surtees was proud and pleased; Ainsworth was helpful and encouraging. On March 2nd he wrote to Surtees enclosing a cheque for the penultimate chapters saying, "He is a glorious fellow and I shall be sorry to see the last of him. But the best of friends must part." At the same time, or just after, he intimated that *Mr. Sponge* must be brought to an end as soon as convenient.

"You must manage," he wrote, "to wind him up in twelve pages, for I have only that space to allot you—not a page more. If therefore you find the matter likely to exceed, you had better leave out any superfluous chapters and reserve them for republication. I have no doubt whatever of the success of the story when brought out with illustrations. It is unquestionably the best sporting tale ever written, and beats Nimrod all to sticks."

When only about eighteen chapters had appeared in the *New Monthly*, Surtees, realizing that at last he had written a success, began to negotiate for its appearance in volume form. He first tried Rudolph Ackermann, but Ackermann was discouraged by the comparative failure of the earlier books and disinclined to take the risk. Messrs. Bradbury and Evans were more far-sighted and agreed to bring it out in one volume with illustrations. They suggested that the book needed some "pruning" to make it acceptable in volume form, and Surtees, accommodating for once, agreed. "It requires considerable pruning and trimming," he wrote, "but there is the substance for a good sporting tale, which Mr. Leech's illustrations will, I think, make sell. It should be ready about the middle of October or so." But some months later, Mr. Frederick Evans, the senior partner of Bradbury and Evans, suggested that the book would command a better circulation if it were first issued in twelve monthly parts at a shilling each with coloured illustrations and woodcuts by Leech, and once more Surtees agreed.

Leech was at the time one of the busiest and most successful illustrators in England, but Thackeray's introduction was enough to commend Surtees to him, and the arrangement was made. Leech himself was delighted with *Mr. Sponge* and especially about the idea of issuing it in monthly parts.

"Mr. Evans," he wrote to Surtees, "has just written to me about the newly proposed form of *Mr. Sponge* which I think excellent and admirably adapted to the work. I presume he will commence with the New Year, and as there are to be twelve coloured illustrations and *red* is a very taking colour with our craft, I write this to say that I think it will be well to have as many hunting ones in the twelve as we can, leaving non-hunting subjects for the wood-cuts."

Throughout the production of the work Surtees and Leech worked together in the most perfect harmony, suggesting ideas to each other, consulting about colours and commiserating about the eccentricities of the printers. The science of colour-printing at that time was imperfectly understood, and Leech suffered much from the distortion of his ideas.

"That our friend Sponge," he wrote to Surtees, "has lost the hair from the top of his head is no fault of mine. It ought to have been coloured like the rest, and was in my pattern. But I assure you the colourers are troublesome customers—a green horse or a blue man would not shock them if they imagined that there ought to be, for the sake of variety, those colours in a picture. For S's tops I laid in the darkest mahogany colour, and not only that, but made a marginal note that they were to be kept *very* brown throughout. But they don't care. . . ." But these were minor irritations. Surtees and Leech understood one another, and between them they produced that rare thing, an illustrated novel where the author and artist are in perfect accord. The success of their efforts was soon assured and the sales of the novel soon rose to a very satisfactory height and remained there. When Colburn in 1843 issued *Handley Cross* in monthly parts, he sold four thousand of the first part, but the sales fell immediately and of none of the succeeding parts were more than four thousand printed. Bradbury and Evans printed and sold five thousand of the first part of *Mr. Sponge*. Part II only ran to four thousand five hundred, but Part III rose to five thousand five hundred, and none of the remaining parts sold less than six thousand. It was the year 1852, and Surtees was forty-seven. He had been writing for twenty-three years and he had arrived at last.

IV

Most of Surtees' letters to Leech at the end of 1851 are dated from Belford, where he was hunting, as he so often did, with Lord Elcho's hounds. It seems to have been his custom every winter to spend several weeks hunting there, and in Lord Elcho's absence to take charge of the hounds. They were great friends; and when the single-volume edition was in preparation in 1852, it was to Lord Elcho that Surtees asked permission to dedicate it.

> MY DEAR LORD [he wrote on the sixth of September],
>
> I take the liberty of asking the following favour: I have long been desirous of accrediting a work to the first sportsman of the day but have never felt that I have produced anything worthy of so distinguished an honour.
>
> Public opinion, however, having declared strongly in favour of *Mr. Sponge*, I venture to ask to be allowed to dedicate the volume in some such terms as the following:
>
> To the Right Honble Lord Elcho
>
> In gratitude for many seasons of excellent sport with his hounds on the Border, this volume is with his kind permission inscribed by his obliged and faithful servant
>
> The Author.
>
> If you have read the work of which I requested the publishers to send you an early copy every month, you will perhaps be surprized at my making such a characterless character as Mr. Sponge the hero, but the fact is the work was written to decry the steeple

chase, the betting-list system, and winds up with one of those sorry exhibitions.

The modesty of Sponge is borrowed from a certain free and easy acquaintance of ours.

Trusting that this will find your Lordship in the full health of hard exercise, looking forward, as I am, to the days of November :

I have the honour, etc.

We would gladly know who was the certain free and easy acquaintance from whom Mr. Sponge took his origin, but the identity has never been revealed. It is difficult to identify, as Mr. Cuming does, Lord Scamperdale with that Sir William Chaytor of Wilton Castle who is supposed to have been the original of Thackeray's Sir Pitt Crawley. Mr. Cuming says that " The family likeness between Thackeray's Sir Pitt Crawley in *Vanity Fair* and Surtees' Lord Scamperdale in *Mr. Sponge's Sporting Tour* must have been remarked by all who are familiar with the two novels." He adduces in evidence Surtees' autograph book, in which is a letter from Sir William Chaytor endorsed in pencil with the words " The Original of Sir Pitt Crawley in Thackeray's *Vanity Fair*." " Surtees," Mr. Cuming adds, " knew Sir William Chaytor, and Surtees never hesitated to make friends and acquaintances thus serve his literary ends." But the parallel between Lord Scamperdale and Sir Pitt Crawley is anything but probable. Sir Pitt was no sportsman. He was in Thackeray's own words " a cunning, mean, selfish, foolish, disreputable old man." He was a " stickler for his dignity while at home and seldom drove out but with four horses and though he dined off boiled mutton, had always three footmen to serve it."

Lord Scamperdale was neither cunning, mean nor foolish, and not particularly selfish nor at all disreputable. Neither had he anything in common with Sir Pitt in the matter of personal dignity. When he went abroad he rode or drove himself in a trap accompanied only by Jack Spraggon. There were no footmen in his house, and when he dined at home his favourite " tripe and cow-heel " was slammed down on the table by the butler or a slatternly maid. On the rare occasions when they drank wine, Jack Spraggon was sent to the cellar to fetch it. Sir Pitt was " such a sharp landlord that he could hardly find any but bankrupt tenants," but if Mr. Springwheat is a fair sample of Lord Scamperdale's tenants, then Lord Scamperdale was anything but a poor landlord. Surely the final disproof is that Thackeray says of Sir Pitt that " he lost

Lord Scamperdale in his best clothes

[MR. SPONGE'S SPORTING TOUR]

more horses than any man in the country from underfeeding and buying cheap." Lord Scamperdale doubtless bought cheap when he got the chance, but he was the last man in the world to keep worthless horses or to underfeed what horses he kept. Apart from a certain boorishness and indifference to personal comfort and adornment there is in truth little resemblance between the two. We may accept Surtees' pencilled note about Sir William Chaytor without in any way connecting it with the creation of Lord Scamperdale.

It is clear that Surtees was delighted with *Mr. Sponge*'s success, for in his letter to Lord Elcho we find it stated that public opinion had declared strongly in favour of the book, and that he himself felt that it was worthy of dedication to "the first sportsman of the day." Lord Elcho had filled the vacancy in Surtees' esteem left by the death of Mr. Lambton. The one-volume edition was published in 1853 with illustrations by Leech and proved as successful as the previous edition in monthly parts. The book has always been his most widely read work with the possible exception of *Handley Cross*: and *Handley Cross* is more often quoted than read. It was the only work up to date to be published in America, where it appeared in 1856 and again in 1859. And it has the supreme distinction of having been translated into French and published in France. In 1925 M. Adolphe Le Goupy of Boulevard de la Madeleine, Paris, brought out a French edition under the somewhat forbidding title of *La Tournée Sportive de Mr. Sponge* par R. S. Surtees, auteur de *Handley Cross*, *Les Villégiatures de Jorrocks*, etc., etc. Traduit de l'Anglais par Lionel Philippe, illustré de 60 croquis et 10 aquarelles par Harry Elliott. Mr. Sponge no doubt would have appreciated the compliment. But what, one wonders, would Lord Scamperdale and Jack Spraggon have said about it?

It was in 1853, the year of *Mr. Sponge*'s appearance in one volume, that the inevitable explosion occurred between Surtees and Ainsworth. Directly *Mr. Sponge* came to an end in the *New Monthly Magazine* in 1851 Ainsworth accepted *Young Tom Hall, his Heartbreaks and Horses* to follow it. Surtees had originally wanted it to run as a serial in *Punch*, of which his old colleague Mark Lemon was then editor and for which Leech was doing much of the illustrating.

His idea had been to have it published in weekly numbers with Leech's illustrations, but Lemon hesitated and finally declined it. He liked the work but felt unable to allot weekly space for so long ahead to a work of purely sporting interest. *Punch*'s public was not predominantly sporting and its editor could call on practically any comic writer whom he liked to name. Surtees was disappointed but, being anxious to follow up the success of *Mr. Sponge*, he urged it upon Bradbury and Evans as a "serial say in twelve monthly parts." They were quite willing to publish it but, being then busy with the preparation of *Mr. Sponge*, suggested deferring its publication in volume form until it had run its course as a serial in a first-class magazine. Ainsworth was anxious to have it for the *New Sporting*, and as *Mr. Sponge* had come to an end in April 1851, *Tom Hall* began in October of the same year. It must be repeated, as from that cause the quarrel sprang, that Surtees had stipulated that the book must appear anonymously and that Ainsworth, though reluctantly, had agreed.

At first, as we have seen, all went well. *Tom Hall* was popular, Surtees and Ainsworth were on friendly terms, and in November they had agreed that *Tom Hall* should run for another six months.

At the beginning of December a *New Monthly Magazine* advertisement mentioned Robert Smith Surtees by name as the author of *Tom Hall*. It is impossible to excuse Ainsworth. He had been made aware from the very start of the previous work, *Mr. Sponge*, that the maintaining of Surtees' anonymity was a condition of his works being published. He was reminded of it when *Tom Hall* was accepted when Surtees wrote the words already quoted. "I find I can write much better and with far more pleasure to myself when I am free to deny authorship if I like." It was well known in the literary world that Surtees' anonymity was to him what her virginity is to a woman. Ainsworth could not plead ignorance, nor did he try—but his plea that the advertisement had been inserted by mistake is singularly unconvincing. He was the proprietor and editor of the magazine, and if such an advertisement had been inserted without his knowledge and approval it must have been by a most exceptional oversight. It seems more probable that Ainsworth had connived at, if not ordered, its publication. He had, as we know, a profound belief in the value of a good name in an advertisement, and he had, too, a liking for his own way.

But so had Surtees, and his reaction was swift and decisive. On 28th December, he wrote to Ainsworth :

Dear Sir,

I cannot permit the use you are making of my name and must request you will immediately withdraw it from the *New Monthly* advertisement.

Yours truly—R. S. Surtees.

The tone is peremptory, but there is every reason for it. There had been a plain and open agreement on the subject, and Ainsworth had violated it. Surtees was not the man to pass over any breach of an agreement, especially of one on a subject about which he felt so strongly. Ainsworth hastily withdrew the advertisement, but the curtness of Surtees' tone stung him. As he was to write later, it was not made in terms consistent with their previous correspondence. But what probably stung him still more was the knowledge that he had been caught out either in a gross blunder or in an act of dishonesty. Some rankling in his Nonconformist Mancunian conscience must have prompted his reply, which not only matched Surtees in brevity, but took an unworthy revenge :

> SIR [he wrote on 1st January 1852]
>
> I beg to enclose cheque on Coutts and Co. for £6 in payment for the present chapters of *Tom Hall*. I shall be glad if you will wind up the tale as soon as you conveniently can.
>
> Your faithful servant,
>
> WILLIAM HARRISON AINSWORTH.

No man who was not perfectly well aware that he was in the wrong would have written that. And no man, least of all a man of Surtees' temperament, could be expected to put up with it. Surtees replied at once :

> SIR,
>
> I beg to acknowledge the receipt of your note and cheque for the January portion of *Hall*, which it is not my intention to continue.
>
> Yours obediently,
>
> R. S. SURTEES.

Ainsworth had gone too far and he knew it. His request to Surtees to wind up the tale as soon as convenient had been intended as a slap in the face, and Surtees' reply landed like a fist on the point of his chin. He did not want to lose *Tom Hall*, which was proving as popular as had *Mr. Sponge*, but by his ill-temper and tactlessness he had brought the loss on himself. Like all his type, he had to try and justify himself and to put his opponent in the wrong. The day he received Surtees' note he wrote :

Sir,

I have to acknowledge the receipt of your letter announcing your intention of discontinuing *Tom Hall* in the magazine. I do not think this fair to the magazine or to me. But I have no wish that the tale should be continued.

In closing the correspondence, I must remark that the courtesy and consideration with which you have always been treated by me during your somewhat lengthened connection with the *New Monthly* ought in my opinion to have rendered your present communication and that which preceded it less abrupt. I was very sorry that the advertisement occasioned you annoyance, but I had not the slightest idea that it could do so. On your request it was immediately withdrawn: and if this request had been made in terms consistent with our previous intercourse, I should have felt no occasion for further remark—except to express regret at any unintentional interference on my part with your other arrangements, if such was the case.

Your obedient Servant,

William Harrison Ainsworth.

One can only feel that with this letter Ainsworth made the worst of a bad case. When a man writes of the "courtesy and consideration" which he has shown to another it is fully evident that his conscience is troubling him. Ainsworth tried to put the blame on Surtees' abruptness, but his remark that he had not the slightest idea that the advertisement could cause Surtees annoyance is sheer nonsense. Surtees had made it clear that he insisted on anonymity both for *Mr. Sponge* and for *Tom Hall*. His letter, which is a clear proof of it, must have been in the *New Monthly* offices.

It was the end of their intercourse. Surtees very sensibly did not answer the letter, and they never spoke to each other again. But the tragedy is that it was also the end of *Tom Hall*. Surtees never finished the book, though it promised to be one of his best and most entertaining works. He thriftily used most of the characters for his next two novels, *Ask Mamma* and *Plain or Ringlets*. Mr. Hall and Tom Hall, Lord Heartycheer and Angelena Blunt, Major Guineafowl and his wife all reappear. But we never hear again of that most eccentric of regiments, the Heavysteed Dragoons, and we never meet Lord Lavender's Yeomanry. Either Surtees had not the heart to finish it or else his publishers advised against it, for Bradbury and Evans attached great importance to a preliminary run as a serial before publication in volume form. A work which had ceased abruptly and without explanation before it had run half its course as a serial would be sadly handicapped from the start.

It is a real loss to the world of fiction, for the work even as it stands to-day is a masterpiece. It is the more serious because the interruption seems to have caused a hesitation and uncertainty for some time in Surtees' work. In *Mr. Sponge* he had found his true form, and in *Tom Hall* he was at the top of it. There is a recession in *Ask Mamma*, good though much of it is, and a lot of *Plain or Ringlets* is tedious and silly. It is not till his last work, *Mr. Facey Romford's Hounds*, that he finds his true form again and writes as he wrote in *Mr. Sponge* and *Tom Hall.*

More than thirty years before, two anonymous friends had caused the destruction of his first attempt at a novel and deprived the world of what might not have been a masterpiece but would certainly have been a work of interest. But *Tom Hall*, as far as it goes, is a masterpiece ; and its cessation must be for ever attributed to the obstinacy and tactlessness of Mr. Harrison Ainsworth.

CHAPTER VI

Full Cry

" How he carries the scent ! and when he loses it, see how eagerly he flings to recover it again ! There now he's at head again ! "—PETER BECKFORD.

" No two men 'gree upon the merits of a run, 'less they 'appen to be the only ones to see it, when they arrange that wot one says t'other shall swear to : your real jealous bouys can't bear to see many at the finish."—*Handley Cross.*

I

" OUR Tom shall be a gentleman." " Our Billy shall be a gentleman." These laudible sentiments expressed by Mr. Hall Senior in *Young Tom Hall* and Mr. Pringle senior in *Ask Mamma* indicate clearly the target at which Surtees' satire was next to be directed. The principal characters of these books that follow *Mr. Sponge* have one thing in common. Neither Tom Hall, Billy Pringle nor Admiration Jack in *Plain or Ringlets* is a gentleman, and all three of them use the hunting field for social advancement. It is natural to think of Tom Hall, Billy Pringle and Jack Bunting—with the possible addition of Jasper Goldspink—together, because they all sprang from the same origin—the ill-fated *Young Tom Hall, his Heartbreaks and Horses.* When the unfortunate collision with Harrison Ainsworth put an end to Tom Hall's career, Surtees never finished the work, but he was too thrifty and perhaps too much in love with his characters to waste them. In one form and another they nearly all reappear in the two succeeding books. Tom Hall himself becomes Billy Pringle and Jasper Goldspink. Old Mr. Hall with his " sivin and four's elivin and twelve is twenty three " is almost unaltered as Mr. Goldspink, senior. Lord Heartycheer and his pander-huntsman, Dicky Thorndyke, become Lord Ladythorne and Dicky Boggledyke. The financial discussions between Mr. Hall and Lord Lavender are revived between Mr. Goldspink and the Duke of Tergiversation. Angelena Blunt is reincarnate in Miss de Glancey, down to the details of that pathetic drenching in a thunderstorm which cost her the regard of her elderly admirer. And the whole idea of the three books is the same—the idea of a young man with more money than sense (though

Admiration Jack had more sense than money and little enough of either) who goes out to hunt for social advancement and also to make himself attractive to the other sex. The other sex, too, is more prominent than in the other books, and much typical Victorian humour—for Surtees it is surprisingly Victorian—is expended on the matrimonial ambitions of Angelena Blunt, the Misses Yammerton and Rosa McDermott.

Inevitably the characters and the incidents lose something by their dilution and dissipation. In the rich comedy of *Young Tom Hall*, unfinished as it is, there is enough material for two good books—but not for three. By the time that Surtees reaches *Plain or Ringlets* the texture has grown thin. The strongest and most interesting characters in the later books are those which are not carried forward from *Tom Hall* but appear for the first time, Sir Moses Mainchance and Cuddy Flintoff in *Ask Mamma*, and Jovey Jessop and Jug Boyston in *Plain or Ringlets*. After *Plain or Ringlets*, Surtees plainly if belatedly feels that he has squeezed the last possible drop of humour out of these situations and characters. He revives the world of Soapey Sponge and ends his work with the triumph of *Facey Romford's Hounds*.

There is in *Tom Hall* a swiftness of movement, an exuberance of humour that recalls *Handley Cross*. It has all the astringent satire of *Mr. Sponge's Sporting Tour* combined with something of the geniality of the Jorrocks Trilogy. There is little geniality in *Ask Mamma*, none in *Plain or Ringlets*, and the satire has a querulous, almost a peevish note which is absent from *Tom Hall* which precedes them or *Facey Romford* which succeeds them. Harrison Ainsworth has much to answer for. He not only interrupted what might have been Surtees' best novel, but he was the cause of a little uncertainty which affected the next two books. There is in them a trace of lack of confidence which does not wholly disappear until Facey Romford recovers all the fun and wholeheartedness of Soapey Sponge. Yet *Ask Mamma* and *Plain or Ringlets* show no lack of technical skill. They have all the closeness of texture and singleness of purpose that distinguished *Mr. Sponge* and that were absent from *Hawbuck Grange* and the Jorrocks books. The narrative is coherent in all of them, and the twin themes of hunting and courtship are closely interwoven. The stories depend on the central characters, and there is no feeling that incidents are strung on the thread of a weak character as *Hawbuck Grange* hangs on the colourless Tom Scott. Almost any chapter or chapters can be extracted from *Hawbuck Grange*, *Handley Cross* or *Hillingdon Hall* and read separately without detriment to them

Cuddy Flintoff

[ASK MAMMA]

or to the rest of the work. It is plain that the novels from *Mr. Sponge* onwards were conceived as single, whole works, whereas the previous books had been collected magazine extracts. *Tom Hall,* it is true, ran as a serial in the *New Monthly*, but it is as coherent and fluent as any of the later books and could have been published in volume form without any alteration. The other two books were written for publication in volume form though, as was the custom of the time, they were both first issued in monthly parts. *Ask Mamma* was issued by Bradbury and Evans in thirteen monthly parts from 1857 to 1858, with Leech's illustrations, and published in one volume in 1858. *Plain or Ringlets*, which was dedicated to the twelve-year-old Anthony Surtees, was also issued by Bradbury and Evans, with Leech's illustrations, in thirteen monthly parts from 1858 to 1860 and published in one volume in 1860. The unfortunate *Tom Hall*, whose career ended in the *New Monthly* in 1853, had to wait till 1926 when Blackwood and Son published it in one volume, edited by Mr. E. D. Cuming, with illustrations by Mr. G. D. Armour.

II

It is difficult to believe that any mess could be quite so corrupt and dissolute as that of the Heavysteed Dragoons. From Colonel Blunt, who spent his spare time playing skittles behind the riding-school with Quartermaster Diddle, and Major Fibs, the shabby horse-dealer, down to the latest joined subaltern, the drunken Cornet Jug, there is not an honest or sober man among them. Individually they are beneath contempt. Together they move through the book with a richly collective humour that makes them irresistible. Even in Surtees' novels there is no incident more exuberantly joyous than the arrival of the Dragoons in their drag to hunt with Lord Heartycheer's hounds. And even among his list of entertainments and parties, there is nothing to compare with Colonel Blunt's *Thé Dansant*. Colonel Blunt himself was obviously, as was Surtees' habit, taken from an acquaintance of his own, for Ainsworth wrote to him, "I suppose you had T—— in mind." And his daughter Angelena is the only female character except Lucy Glitters on whom Surtees expends any real care. Even so, he is not very successful with her. She shares with Lucy Glitters her skill in horsemanship, but beyond that she has little personality of her own. Her manœuvres to secure a husband, supported as they are by the skill of her mother and the

The Hunt Ball – "Ask Mamma" Polka

well-intentioned blunders of her father, are poor and conventional fun, the very stuff of contemporary Victorian humour. The hero of the book, Young Tom Hall himself, is a fat, foolish youth who wanted to be a gentleman without, like Mr. Sponge, knowing how and who hunted because he thought it was the thing to do, though he was genuinely terrified of horses and anything to do with them. He is too much a passive figure to have any interest as a comic character, and what little claim to sympathy he ever possessed he loses by the senseless brutality of his riding, which killed his horse in the last chapter of the unfinished work. Major Fibs has all Mr. Sponge's cupidity and dishonesty in the matter of horseflesh without any of his gay impudence to relieve it. But the triumphant figure of the book is Colonel Blunt, the commanding officer of the Heavysteed Dragoons. In his gross person and his gauche manners he epitomizes all Surtees' hatred of the cavalry officer, yet there is something magnificent about him, something that for a fleeting moment almost recalls Mr. Jorrocks. He was a rogue and snob and a skinflint where Mr. Jorrocks was none of them, but he had about him something of the indestructibility, the resilience that distinguished the Master of the Handley Cross Hounds. With every turn of fortune and chance of fate against him, he refuses to be quite subdued. Even Lord Heartycheer's frigidity cannot chill that sublime impertinence that begins with his greeting " 'Ow are ye, Heartycheer ? " on their first meeting. Colonel Blunt, ill-dressed, impecunious, only half-sober, arrives at the meet of Lord Heartycheer's hounds with his motley crew of officers, all worse than ill-dressed and less than half-sober, and carries off the meeting with a shameless and gross insolence that has a touch of greatness about it. Mrs. Blunt, his wife, is worthy of him—as common as Mrs. Jorrocks, as designing as Mrs. Flather, as shameless as Mrs. Pringle, as calculating as Mrs. McDermott yet with a spark of vitality in her that none of them possesses. There is something almost heroic in the utter shamelessness of her efforts on behalf of her daughter that redeems that conventional Victorian idea of fun. Colonel and Mrs. Blunt are a pretty pair of rogues, but they share one great merit—they are abundantly alive.

III

The real strength of *Ask Mamma* lies not in the characters imported from *Tom Hall* but in those that now appear for the first time—Cuddy Flintoff, Major Yammerton and Sir Moses Mainchance. It is a pity that we see so little of Cuddy, a rogue and a humbug so thorough-paced as almost to be endearing. He is a type with which followers of any sport will be familiar—a sportsman whose achievements are all in the past or in the imagination and who makes up for present lack of performance by a ceaseless use of sporting language and imagery.

"Cuddy was an 'all-about' sportsman, who professed to be of all hunts but blindly went to none. Cuddy's sporting was in the past tense, indeed he seemed to exist altogether upon the recollection of the chase, which must have made a lively impression upon him, for he was continually interlarding his conversation with view holloas, yoicks wind 'ims! yoicks push him ups! Indeed in walking about he seemed to help himself along with the aid of for-rards on! for-rards on! so that a person out of sight but within hearing would think he was hunting a pack of hounds.

"He dressed the sportsman, too, most assiduously, bird's-eye cravats, step-collared, striped vests, green or Oxford grey cutaways, with the neatest-fitting trousers on the best bow-legs that ever were seen." Cuddy was a hanger-on of Sir Moses Mainchance, staying in his house, drinking his brandy, but never hunting with his hounds.

When the servants arrived with the bedroom candles "Cuddy suddenly turned whipper-in, and working his right arm as if he were cracking a whip, kept holloaing, 'get away hoick! get away hoick! until he drove Billy and Baronet and all before him." Only once in the book did they get Cuddy on to a horse, and that was to ride in the wholly ridiculous steeplechase against Billy Pringle's valet, Monsieur Jean Rougier. Rougier, whose real name was Jack Rogers, is another of Surtees' insufferable servants, and had been already hinted at in *Young Tom Hall* in the person of Tights or Captain de Roseville. In *Ask Mamma* he is developed at unnecessary length, and he remains as a memorial of Surtees' lifelong conviction of the entire futility of all Frenchmen. In his youth he had been a postillion, and he remembered enough of his horsemanship to beat Cuddy Flintoff across country, no very difficult feat, for Cuddy was, as Sir Moses said, "an afternoon sportsman—he's greatest after dinner."

Major Yammerton, "Five-and-thirty years Master of Haryers without a subscription," though a prosy and pompous little man and not over-scrupulous in the matter of horse-dealing, had many merits. Like all Surtees' currant-jelly boys, he hunted well and seriously, and if he boasted about his achievements, they were at any rate, unlike Cuddy

Flintoff's, actual and not only reminiscent. He had a foolish wife and three marriageable daughters all of whom fancied Billy Pringle, and one of whom eventually became Lady Mainchance. He sold to Billy Pringle that worthless animal Napoleon the Great; but there are few honest horse-dealers in Surtees' works, and Billy was like Mr. Sponge's friend Waffles, "such an ass that he deserved to be done." And done he was, first by Major Yammerton and subsequently by Sir Moses Mainchance.

Major Yammerton had other interests beside hunting and horse-dealing. He was a serious farmer, kept a herd of excellent cows and was an enthusiast for land drainage. Except for the unpublished "Description of Durham," we have not heard anything of Surtees' agricultural views and activities since *Hillingdon Hall.* In *Ask Mamma* they reappear with both Major Yammerton and Sir Moses Mainchance. At the end of the book they join forces after Sir Moses marries Clara Yammerton, and the Major displaces Mr. Mordecai Nathan as manager of Sir Moses' property. He introduces his favourite drainage improvements and "promises to set the water-works playing at Pangburn Park just as he did at Yammerton Grange." Surtees calls him "an improving landlord," and in this respect he is the exact opposite of Sir Moses Mainchance, whose only object in buying a country estate was to give himself consequence, and who tried to wring the last halfpenny out of his tenants. Surtees, himself a landlord and a practising farmer, knew the truth of the immemorial saying that you can only get out of the land what you put into it. Sir Moses was what might be expected from his lineage—his great-grandfather sold penknives, dog-collars and street sponges, his grandfather sold old clothes, rhubarb and gum arabic, his father combined a curiosity shop with a money-lending business. Sir Moses himself sold the family concerns, bought a baronetcy, and set up as a country gentleman and a master of foxhounds. The result was inevitable. "Sir Moses' property went rapidly back and soon became a sort of last refuge for the destitute, whither the ejected of all other estates congregated prior to scattering their stock, on failing to get farms in more favoured localities. As they never meant to pay, of course, they all offered high rents, and then, having got possession . . . they could 'make nout on't at that rent!' Nor could they have made aught on them if they had had them for nothing, seeing that their capital consisted solely of their intense stupidity. Then if Sir Moses wouldn't reduce the rent he might just do his 'warst,' meanwhile they pillaged the land both by day and by night. The cropping of course corresponded with the tenure, and may be described as just anything they could get off the land. White crop succeeded white crop, if the weeds didn't smother the seeds, or if any of the slovens did 'try for a few turnips,' as they called it, they were sown on dry spots selected here and there, with an implement resembling a dog's-meat man's wheelbarrow—drawn by one ass and steered by another."

The tirade is violent, for good farming lay very near to Surtees' countryman's heart. But if he is severe he is also just, and much as he loathes Sir Moses, he distributes the blame impartially between him and his tenants. Every evil of small-holding farmers which is touched on in the "Description of Durham" is represented on Sir Moses' estate. There are farmers like Henerey Brown and Co. with insufficient capital, like Jacky Hindmarch with insufficient labour. There are Turnbull, Gowk and Heavyheels who have neither capital nor labour and whose one idea of farming is begging from their landlord. There are the evils of starving the land of lime and manure, of persisting with arable farming at the expense of pasture-land, and the supreme evil of lack of drainage. "Altogether they are a wonderful breed! It will hardly be credited hereafter, when the last of these grubbing old earthworms is extinct, that in this anxious, commercial, money-striving country, where every man is treading on his neighbour's heels for cash, that there should have been a race of men who required all the coaxing and urging and patting on the back to induce them to benefit themselves that these slugs of small tenant farmers have done. And the bulk of them not a bit better for it." Finally he dismisses them collectively as "weasels." "The thing is to get rid of the weasels and with public companies framed for draining, building, doing everything that is required without that terrible investigation of title, no one is justified in keeping his property in an unproductive state. The fact is that no man of capital will live in a cottage, the thing therefore is to lay a certain number of these small holdings together, making one good farm of them all with suitable buildings and, as the saying is, let the weasels go to the wall. They will be far happier and more at home with spades or hoes in their hands, than in acting a part for which they have neither capital. courage nor capacity." It is a drastic solution, though perhaps a reasonable one, but it was not the solution which commended itself to Sir Moses Mainchance. His only answer to the problem was to discharge his agent, Mr. Teaser, and to appoint in his place "that promising swell, young Mr. Mordecai Nathan, of Cursitor Street, whose knowledge of the country consisted in having assisted in the provincial department of his father's catchpoll business in the glorious days of writs and sponging-houses." But Mr. Nathan, as was only to be expected, was no more successful than Mr. Teaser. Henerey Brown and Co. were too much for him. Having sold their horses and all their stock, they left a note "hanging to the key in the house-door, saying that they had gone to Horseterhaylia, where Sir Moses needn't trouble to follow them." It was not until Major Yammerton displaced Mr. Nathan that Sir Moses' estate began to prosper.

It was Sir Moses Mainchance's misfortune to combine in his own person the characteristics of all those classes of society whom Surtees most disliked. He was a Jew, a dealer in horses, a pinching landlord, a would-be country gentleman and a cheese-paring master of hounds. It is obvious that Surtees disliked him more than any other character of his creation, and allowed him hardly a redeeming feature. Sir Moses is no more unscrupulous in the matter of horses than the Gentiles, Mr. Sponge and Mr. Romford, no worse a master of hounds than Sir Harry Scattercash, no more offensive a parody of a country gentleman than Mr. Marmaduke Muleygrubs. But where each of them excel in one particular department of roguery or pretentiousness, Sir Moses excels in them all. And he is certainly the worst landlord in any of the books. It cannot be denied that his imperfections of all sorts sprang, in Surtees' opinion, from the common source of his Jewish origin. He is almost the only character of them all to whom Surtees makes no attempt to be fair and, coming from one so fundamentally fair as Surtees was, it argues a depth of dislike beyond the ordinary. And yet Surtees, as we have observed, was no moralist. He does not feel called upon to reward virtue and to punish vice as did his contemporaries. Sir Moses comes to no bad end. He is even allowed his temporary triumph over those early black marketeers Mrs. Margerum, Mr. Gallon and Anthony Thom. And finally he marries Miss Clara Yammerton, whose father begins to rescue his estate from the ruin caused by bad farming and grasping landlordship.

So *Ask Mamma* ends somewhat like a fairy story or a pantomime with everyone—except Billy Pringle—married and likely to live happy every after. Jack gets his Jill, Lord Ladythorne marries Mrs. Pringle, Sir Moses Mainchance marries Clara, Imperial John marries Miss de Glancey, Miss Flora Hammerton marries the Woolpack. And Surtees, a satirical but on the whole a kindly fairy godmother, takes leave of them in a closing speech and with a final toast.

" So let us leave our hero open. And as we have only aimed at nothing but the natural throughout, we will finish by proposing a toast that will include as well the mated and the single of our story, as the mated and the single all the world over, namely, the old and popular one of 'The single married, and the married happy !' drunk with three times three and one cheer more ! HOO-RAY ! "

IV

Plain or Ringlets is an oddity. It is the least amusing and least satisfactory of all the novels, yet it has moments of superlative merit. The discrepancy between old garment and new cloth, between the remnants of *Tom Hall* and the rich new material of Jovey Jessop and Jug Boyston are more apparent than in *Ask Mamma* and the stitching that joins them together is sometimes little better than amateurish cobbling. *Tom Hall* was a magnificent piece of cloth and it made up again very well into *Ask Mamma*, but it has worn very thin by this time.

But to make the garment yet more of a patchwork there are the first twenty-five chapters which again are entirely fresh material, but of a quality and a sort which we have not yet met in Surtees, and happily never meet again. Every artist experiments as long as he lives, and it is obvious in these chapters not only that Surtees was experimenting but that he was driven to the experiment by two distinct motives. He seems to have realized the lack of feminine interest in his novels and to have determined this time to supply it at any cost to himself or his readers. And he seems, too, to have resolved to write a book without any hunting in it. Happily his resolve weakens at Chapter XXVI when we meet Jock Haggish and his hounds, and on the first of November the book comes alive and lives gloriously to the end. But if, after a study of the preceding novels, there is need of any further proof of the fact that Surtees was a supremely good sporting novelist and nothing else, that he is an expert in the hunting field and an amateur away from it, *Plain or Ringlets* abundantly supplies that proof.

The hero of the book, Mr. Bunting, who was known as Admiration Jack, is an unattractive creature. He is supposed to be the owner of a castle in Scotland and to be looking for an heiress to share it with him. He is extremely vain of his dress and personal appearance. He hunts a little but knows nothing about horses. But there is nothing definite about him. He has all Tom Scott's nebulosity without his simplicity and modesty. In fact he is neither one thing nor the other—neither wholly rogue like Sponge and Romford, nor fool like Hall and Pringle, nor honest man like Jorrocks and Scott. He meanders through the book, admiring his waistcoats and his whiskers, and at the end we hardly know and certainly do not care whether he has his castle and finds his heiress or not.

His rival, Jasper Goldspink, is no more interesting—a fat and foolish youth who, like his begetter Tom Hall, hunts for show, hates it and rides abominably. He gets his Rosa in the end and it serves them both right. She married him for his father's money, but Goldspink's Bank failed so she would have been better off with Mr. Bunting, whose estate in Scotland turns out to be of more value than at one time seemed likely. Mr. Bunting read of the marriage and the breaking of the bank " at his highland home—where the reader will be happy to hear that the barrenness of the surface of his property is amply atoned for by the richness of the minerals below—prodigious beds of iron-stone, coal and lime being found on the spot." But in truth by this time the average reader will care very little what happens to either Jasper Goldspink or Admiration Jack.

His Grace the Duke of Tergiversation, whom we first met in *Hawbuck Grange*, is a typical Surtees aristocrat, who hunts and shoots, entertains with splendour, and is at perpetual loggerheads with Mr. Goldspink, his banker. And his distinguished guest, Prince Pirouetteza, is the final incarnation of Surtees' old friend of Brighton days, Baron Gablenz, though Gablenz was a real baron and Pirouetteza was not a real prince. " Our Prince would not have fared quite so well had it been known that he was only the son of a an impudent dancing master at Florence. Hence his agility with his toes. Indeed he would have made a fortune if he had followed the paternal profession, for he was a natural dancer . . . but being just in the morning of life, with a little money left to him by an uncle, he thought it would be far better to dance on terms of equality, and take whatever good the gods might provide. So he dubbed himself a Prince and proceeded to enact the part." But whether he is dancing, shooting, or hunting he is altogether a buffoon, and he perpetuates more than Surtees' friend Gablenz. He is the embodiment of those days at Boulogne and Samer and of what the young Surtees had remarked there, the foreigners' entire lack of perception of the importance of sport.

Mr. Jovey Jessop, when at last he appears (in Chapter XLIV) looks back beyond Boulogne and Samer to the early days at Hamsterley and to the boy who hunted with his father's and Mr. Lambton's hounds. Surtees had never forgotten his early training in the hunting field, first with harriers then with foxhounds. "Mr. Jessop began with that 'best of instructors' a pack of harriers, and having mastered the rudiments of scent, as much as that puzzling phenomenon can be mastered (for after all is said and done all the learning in the world will not make a scent), he gave his harriers away and took to foxhounds."

Once more Surtees uses the device of a ball to collect all his characters together for the final pairing-off. The ball is at Tergiversation Castle, and they are all there—Mr. O'Dicey and Sir Felix Flexible, Mr. and Mrs. Bowderoukins, Admiration Jack and Jasper Goldspink, Mr. Jessop and his Jug. "And what a swell old Tom is himself, fine new, blue coat with a velvet collar and bright buttons, white vest, new nankins with shiney shoes and open-clocked gauze silk stockings. He looks quite respectable and really by no means ugly." But he does not fare well in the pairing-off, for he marries that designing and determined widow, Mrs. McDermott. "Beware o' widders," said the elder Mr. Weller, and Jug Boyston would have done better to beware of Mrs. McDermott, for it was not a happy marriage. "The Jug, we are sorry to say, is not so comfortable as we could wish. Mrs. Boyston stints him of his drink, won't let him dine in his slippers and wants him to make Billy Rough'un go in the coal-cart. She also threatens him with the terrors of Sir Cresswell for desertion and cruelty—beating her on the preterpluperfect part of her person with a boot-jack." Rosa McDermott had little better luck than her mother, for she married Jasper Goldspink, and when the bank failed the old and young Goldspinks live together, "illustrating the truth of the old saying that there was never yet a house built big enough to hold two families." So she ends with her hair in ringlets, the fashion which Jasper preferred. Had she married Admiration Jack she would have worn it plain and shared in the profits of a joint stock company for working the royalties of his Highland estate. Financially she would have been better off, but in the matter of tedium there is little to choose between her two suitors, or in fact between them and Miss Rosa herself. We say good-bye without regret to nearly every character in the book, hoping only that Mr. Jessop soon provided himself with a new Jug and that Mr. and Mrs. Boyston eventually arrived at a *modus vivendi*.

V

If *Plain or Ringlets* is not a successful novel it has its value as a piece of social history. Being less concerned with the hunting field than most of the books, its scope is wider, and during the course of it, Surtees takes a glance at the general scene of Victorian society in the middle of the nineteenth century. He views it with no unfriendly eye, but we are left with the impression that the world was not what it was when he was young.

On the whole it is a fair and not unfavourable summing-up, always remembering that he is not writing about hunting, a sphere in which he noticed an unquestionable decline. But in the country at large he finds much to praise, and he ascribes nearly all the improvements to the spread of the railways. He had changed very early in life from his instinctive dislike of an innovation to the appreciation of a real convenience and amenity. In all the books from *Handley Cross* onwards he speaks gratefully and approvingly of them, and in *Plain or Ringlets* he calls them " The grand, the crowning benefit of all." " Without them," he writes, " cheap postage, cheap papers, cheap literature, extended post-offices would have been inefficient, for the old coaches would never have carried the quantity of matter modern times have evoked." " Thanks to George Stephenson, George Hudson, and the many other Georges who invested their talents and valuable money in the invaluable undertakings, railways have brought wealth and salubrity to everyone's door." And, true countryman that he was, he extols that most elementary of childish delights when travelling, looking out of the window. " Some people say that they have seen the country until they are tired of it and know all the views and scenery on the line. True, but that is not making any allowance for the change produced by the seasons, the birds, the leaves, the hay, the grass, the corn, the ' tormots,' the sowing, the reaping, the stacking. A railway ride presents a rapid panorama of agriculture : a passenger sees the transition from good to bad farming, from good to bad land, from drained to undrained soil, in a quick, forcible unmistakable way, provided he will but look." And the great benefit of the railways is that they make people less insular, less parochial in outlook.

" Independently of the saving of time, railways may be looked upon as downright promoters of longevity, for assuredly a man can do and see twice as much as he formerly could without, so, if Squire Mistletoe lives to seventy or eighty, he will be entitled to have put on his monument that he died at a hundred and forty or a hundred and sixty, as the case may be. Squire Mistletoe can run up to town fifty times for once that his father did, and feel all the better instead of the worse for the trip."

Among the minor benefits he includes cheap books and cheap newspapers. "The books look so new and gay, and above all are so cheap—a shilling for what used to cost a guinea a few years ago. One of the peculiarities of modern travel is the great demand there is for books, a book to prevent people seeing the country being quite as essential as a bun to prevent their being hungry." And of newspapers he writes, "What a wonderful institution is *The Times* ! It is a perfect modern miracle. It has kept increasing for the last five-and-twenty years, till it is nearly the size of the table-cloth on which it is laid every morning at breakfast time. No one feels fit to confront his fellow-men until he has mastered its leading contents. Through its medium every wish may be announced, and every want supplied. The second column of the supplement contains hints for a hundred novels." He contrasts it with the days of small expensive news-sheets when *The Times* was in its infancy and *Punch* not yet born.

"There was no *Punch* in those days to supply the weekly stock of fun, and the papers were small and deficient of news. No family breakfast table-cloth-like sheets, with information from all parts of the globe. But if the size was small, the price was large ; sevenpence being charged some forty years ago for a four-columned London paper of four pages. A quick reader would skim through one of them in five minutes, for the type was bold and well-leaded. The country papers were worse and contained little but advertisements . . . mixed with murders, inquests and a very slight sprinkling of political and parliamentary news. No wonder that people were thrown on their own and each other's resources for information and amusement. Now every pursuit and calling has its organ, all admirably conducted, and published at very low prices."

Surtees was well qualified to speak of the development of newspapers and periodicals for he had first-hand experience. He had edited the *New Sporting Magazine*, contributed to *Bell's Life*, the "Old" *Sporting* and the *New Monthly*, and he had suggested the creation of *The Field*. But, while he chronicles the benefits of the railways, he is not blind to their defects, and he views with alarm the extravagant methods of some of their directors and their reckless expenditure on such things as decorative stations. That he is not altogether consistent about it may be seen from his descriptions of the Roseberry Rocks and the Golconda stations. "The Roseberry Rocks Station was built quite on the 'money-no-object' principle of the early development of railways—light, lofty, spacious and elegant—with a fine holiday air about it. The white marble stands in the highly decorated refreshment rooms are piled with the most tempting viands, solids, fluids, fruits, sweets of all sorts. Everything looks so nice and fresh, that a stranger helps himself boldly without troubling to enquire when the tarts or the cakes were made—so necessary at some stations where they have always a last week's sandwich or pie ready to foist upon the unwary."

Roseberry Rocks was a pleasure resort, and some liberality of spending on the station was permissible. He is much more severe on the London termini.

"The Golconda Station of the Great Gammon and Spinach Railway, as the reader is—or at all events the shareholders are—well aware was built, as George Robins used to say, 'regardless of expense,' the architect having apparently taken his idea of the edifice from some scene in the *Arabian Nights' Entertainment*. Hence the splendid dividend of two-pence-halfpenny a share, so complacently announced by the Chairman. . . . If poor George Stephenson had ventured to shadow forth such a gigantic structure in the early days of railways, he would have been 'pooh-pooh'd' and requested not to make a fool of himself." Surtees was always an opponent of useless display and extravagance—it was that strain of north country thrift which made him introduce some sensible and necessary economies when he was High Sheriff of Durham. He sums up the case against the railway directors with, "If the majority of railways had been constructed with anything like ordinary prudence and economy, they would have been sources of wealth to the shareholders and the public might have travelled for half what they now do. As it was, it was believed that their resources were boundless and every species of folly and extravagance was indulged in."

The English Inn apparently had not shared in the general benefits conferred by the spread of the railways. Surtees had always been sharply critical of inns ever since that spring in the year 1825 when the Highflyer coach set him down at the door of the White Horse Inn in Fetter Lane. "Anything," he then remarked, "is good enough for a stage-coach passenger." But now in 1860 he looks back and sees that the old coaching inn was at any rate better than its modern counterpart.

The old coaching inn with all its faults was a comfortable place, and after years of touring as a hunting correspondent, his review of them is almost nostalgic. "The large, comfortable, old posting houses that existed prior to railways have all disappeared, or been converted into schools or convents or such like purposes. At one of them a man with horses could live very comfortably during the hunting season." And as instances of first-rate inns he cites the George at Melton, the Station at York and the Bedford at Brighton (three houses which happily still exist to-day). But of the others, he writes, "Those houses have all disappeared, or, if any remain, are dragging out miserable existences with weak, worn-out establishments, women waiters and either antediluvian ostlers or ignorant hobbleboys, fresh at each quarter, who hardly know how to put on a bridle. . . . Third-rate country inns in England are deplorable places. Keen must be the British sportsman, or desperately in love the man who can stay long at one of these gristly, tough-mutton houses for the purpose of hunting or courting, or even for a combination of both." The charges as a rule are as formidable as anything that Mr. Chousey compiled for an anniversary. "Six shillings a bottle, or rather three-quarters of a bottle, of the earthiest sherry, eight shillings a bushel for oats: and servants' keep out of all comprehension." That expenditure touches Surtees, who always hated servants, very nearly. "If they cannot board grooms for a guinea a week, how, let us ask, does it happen that a farm-hind will board a stout ploughman for six shillings a week and make money by it too? It is no advantage to a master to have his servant eating veal cutlets or lamb's fry for breakfast, he wants him fed like his horse for useful work. Sportsmen like touring," he concludes, "and would tour very considerably if they could only get moderately housed at anything like reasonable rates: but the present system is almost a bar to locomotion. It is not that sportsmen object to paying inn bills where the accommodation is good, but that they object to pay the price of good accommodation for very bad."

The last subject on which he comments at some length is the change in women's dress, and particularly the development of the crinoline. The film and the musical comedy have invested the crinoline for us with an aura of nostalgic sentiment, and from the point of view of beauty it has an attraction of its own. But to Surtees, regarding it from the angle of convenience and sense, it was an abomination. "Dress," he writes, "has made a marvellous spring since the introduction of railways. Ladies, whose mothers used to get all their things into a moderate-sized box and a carpet bag, travel with great piano-forte-case-like packages, so numerous that they are obliged to be numbered for fear they forget how many they have. And the more they take, the more they want to take, till each lady looks as if she ought to have a luggage-van to herself. Then, to see them attempt the entry of a moderate-sized carriage: the utter disproportion of the door to the 'object,' as it may well be called, that seeks admission! The absurdity of fashion might be tolerated if it inconvenienced only the wearer: but when one lady extends herself to the size of two, she necessarily takes up the room of two, and must exclude someone else from a seat, . . . The only advantage we see in the absurdity is, that it forms a sort of graduated scale of gentility: the more extravagant a woman is in her hoops, the less inclined we are to think her a lady. It is only the vulgar who go into extremes and make themselves look like curtains to bathing-machines."

Surtees had complained about the development of the crinoline in *Mr. Sponge's Sporting Tour* and he returns to it in *Facey Romford's Hounds*. In *Plain or Ringlets* he calls them "Martello Towers" and "expanded gig umbrellas" and speaks of ladies "with much the air of peacocks striving for port on a windy day." But he was always inclined to be a little peevish on the subject of women. In *Plain or Ringlets* at the Duke of Tergiversation's Ball he makes a general complaint of the "drawing on of gloves, arranging the lace, twirling of hoops, making way for each other to go first—for as it has often been observed, there is more trouble in marshalling a party of justices' wives than a bevy of duchesses."

VI

Perhaps the most illuminating part of *Plain or Ringlets*, especially for the light which it throws upon Surtees himself, is the chapter on Squires new and old. He is writing about his own world, the world of country houses, of horses and hounds, as he once knew it and as he knew it at the time of writing. Once more he traces nearly every improvement in their lot back to the introduction of the railways. To that he attributes the increase in their comfort and their intellectual awakening. "In truth," he writes, "the country gentlemen were a land-locked, leg-tied tribe, before the introduction of railways—coaching was uncomfortable and posting expensive, besides which the journey took such a time. There was no running up to town for a week in those days. It took the best part of a week coming from a remote country to make the journey and recover from the effects of it." They were severely restricted in their interests, which consisted of farming and field-sports, drinking and politics and competitive building. " If Squire Fatfield built a great house Squire Flaggon would follow suit with a bigger, and Squire Jollybuck would cap Squire Flaggon with a larger still." And their hospitality had to match the size of their houses " while the conviviality of the dining-room always found a hearty response in the servants' hall—masters and butlers considering it a reproach to let anyone leave the house sober." . . . " A country house," he concludes severely, " in former days was little better than a great unlicensed inn—everything was taken in that arrived and everybody had to be refreshed that came. We have heard of a gentleman—not an M.P. or a man of large fortune either—whose brewer's bill for a single year amounted to no less a sum than eight hundred pounds." It is a characteristic objection based on a lifelong distaste for extravagance and that strain of personal austerity that was in him.

Surtees was neither spoil-sport nor Puritan, but he had a dislike for excess and especially for excess in wine. We have Nimrod's word for it that there was great wine-drinking at Hamsterley when Surtees was a boy ; it may be that something fastidious in his nature revolted at any excess of this sort and inspired the severity with which he regarded Sir Harry Scattercash, Cuddy Flintoff and their fellows. Jovey Jessop, in *Plain or Ringlets*, who was obviously one of his favourite characters, had drunk deeply till he saw the folly of it and won his way to abstemiousness. But Surtees spares a regret for the passing of the great age of port-drinking. " There was no blowing men out with Champagne or sparkling Moselle during dinner then as there is now : Sherry and Madeira were the regulation wines . . . but the dinner wines were rarely taken into account, the night's consumption being calculated solely on the Port."

On the subject of port he becomes almost lyrical. " In thus noting the manners and customs of a by-gone day, we must not omit to do justice to the merits of the port wine, which certainly was excellent. There was no buying of two dozen hampers in those days ; every man had his stock of port wine in wood as well as in bottle, and that in the wood was not advanced to the bottle before a long probationary process. . . . Port was the staple beverage in those days, fine, clear, ruby-coloured wine, not a headache in a hogshead of it, as the old ones used to say, and certainly they tried it at high pressure."

In 1858, the year of *Plain or Ringlets*, the activities of the new squires were no longer restricted to sport, building and port-drinking. The

"Now I'll have a little"

[PLAIN OR RINGLETS]

railways had opened up easy communications between shire and shire, and between the shires and the towns—particularly between the shires and London. We know from Surtees' own memoirs how fully he availed himself of this convenience and how often he visited London and Brighton. It was at number eighty King's Road, Brighton, that he died in 1864.

In every way the country gentleman's outlook was being enlarged, and in no way more importantly than by the easier access to London. And when he arrived in London he was far better off than in those days of chop-house and coffee-house of which Mr. Jorrocks had so bitterly complained. "The next greatest boon to railways," Surtees continues, "that modern Squires have to be thankful for is the great multiplication of London Clubs." And he calls clubs the greatest and cheapest luxuries of modern times.

The nineteenth century saw the heyday of the London club. They had developed from the coffee-houses of a hundred years before, and passed through the great days of gambling when Charles James Fox played for two nights and a day without a break and the Earl of Sandwich had meat placed between two slices of bread so that he might eat without stopping his play. During the next hundred years clubs sprang up all over London for men with community of interests—the Services, the Universities, the Stage and the Bar, the country and sporting sets. Surtees attributes their growth to the fact that, after the luxury of the new railway travel, men would not be content with the rough-and-ready comfort of the old coaching or new railway inn. "These hotels hold out no inducement for a run up to town for the mere pleasure of the thing. This is what the clubs do. They invite visits. A man feels that he has a real substantial home—a home containing every imaginable luxury, without the trouble of management or forethought—a home that goes on as steadily in his absence as during his presence, to which he has not even the trouble of writing a note to say that he is coming to find everything as comfortable as he left it."

It is a typically male attitude of mind, and no doubt to Surtees one of the main attractions of the London clubs was that, like the hunting field and like his own novels, they were exclusively for his own sex. He does not appear to be interested in what amenities were provided for women in London. Probably he thought that it was better for them to remain quietly in the country. But for men the clubs were to be home without its encumbrances and with an improved menu.

" Talk of country cream, country butter, country eggs, ' our farm of four acres ' and so on : what country house can surpass the butter, cream and eggs of a first-rate London Club ? Not only is the cream good, the butter good and the eggs good, but the whole breakfast apparatus is of the nicest and most inviting order. Everything you want and nothing more. Then the finely flavoured tea is always made with boiling water, instead of the luke-warm beverage we sometimes get : the muffins are fresh, the ham handsomely cut, the rolls crisp and the toast neither leathery nor biscuity. A club breakfast is a meal to saunter over and enjoy, alternately sipping the tea and reading the newspaper."

It is indeed an advance from Mr. Jorrocks's coffee-house breakfast " of a dirty egg, some toasted wedges of bread and a lump of carrion wot the waiter calls beef " ; and at dinner-time, too, from Mr. Jorrocks's " filthy, mustardy, cabbagey cloth," and his " third of a bottle of warm port as a pint."

" The dinners are quite on a par with the breakfasts and adapted to every variety of pocket and appetite. The best of all is that though there is no previous arrangement on the part of the members, everything is as quickly supplied as if there had been. A quarter of an hour suffices to have dinner on the table, soup, fish, meat, sweets and all." Undoubtedly the lot of the " new " squire is better than that of his predecessor of fifty or even thirty years before. But Surtees, who always took country life and its duties seriously, is concerned about the direction in which these luxuries and amenities may lead the squire, whose first care should be his own estate. " The old squires," he writes, " were rich—rich in the fewness of their wants, but the new squires have found wants that their forefathers were ignorant of. The old home manor won't do, they must have a moor : the row on the river won't do, they must have a yacht on the sea : the couple of hunters for Squire Jawleyman's hounds won't do, they must have six and go upon grass."

Already we can see the results of these newly awakened appetites, for in their desire for increased incomes to gratify them the squires are taking to speculation on the stock-exchange and even to trade. " We strongly suspect, however," he comments, " that the squires will find no safer or better speculation than in draining or improving their own land. We do not advocate their teaching the farmers their trade, but we like to see them dispel the prejudices of habit by their example and superior intelligence."

VII

When *Plain or Ringlets* was published Surtees was fifty-five. Even for those days it was no great age, but the Surtees men were not long-lived, and he was within four years of his own death. It is the work, not of an old man, but of a man past his prime, whose thoughts are turning back to his early days and who is beginning to strike a balance between the good and evil that he has seen in his life. Such an account is of great interest for the record of the changes seen in forty years of an active life, but of still greater interest for the light which it throws on the accountant himself; since a man in compiling such a record necessarily shows his own values, his own standards of judgment. And the final value of *Plain or Ringlets,* that curiously uneven work, is the picture that it gives of Robert Smith Surtees towards the end of his life.

It would be an easy but a superficial judgment to write him off as a typical Tory hunting squire, distinguished only from his equals by being more articulate and by what he himself described as "a taste for scribbling." A Tory he undoubtedly was by tradition, by temperament and in politics. But he was no Squire Mistletoe or Squire Flaggon. He had indeed all the virtues of his class, their high sense of duty to their land and their people, their love of sport, their honesty, loyalty and physical courage. But he was without most of their commoner faults, their occasional coarseness, their gross obstinacy and grosser appetites. And above all, Tory as he was, he did not share their determined opposition to anything new. His attitude to any innovation was, as might be expected from him, both fair and sensible. As an innovation he distrusted it, as he distrusted the early railways. If it proved its worth he welcomed it and made no secret of his change of mind. It is a far cry from the railways of the early twenties "whose dirty appearance seemed well adapted to the passengers who travel in them," to those of 1858, "the grand, the crowning benefit of all." In the same way he welcomed improvements in farming, fertilizers and drainage especially, practised them on his own land and extolled them in his novels and in the unpublished "Description of Durham." And how far he was intellectually in advance of his time and his class is evident from his rare remarks about music and the arts. "Whether or not we have recently turned into a military nation," he wrote in 1860, "there can be no doubt that we have greatly advanced as a musical one. There is scarcely a village of any size without its band, and where nothing but cock- and dog-fighting went on, and nothing but Bacchanalian songs were heard, we have now the notes of soft music wafted on the breeze." And he adds the truly advanced opinion that, "We cannot but think that if our legislators were to increase the harmless enjoyments of the people—say throw open the Museums, the Picture Galleries, the Crystal Palace on a Sunday—they would do them far more real service than by burthening them with a troublesome franchise that they do not require." Politically he had never moved from the opinions that he expressed at Gateshead in 1837 when he wrote, "The Franchise I consider sufficiently low to place it within the Reach of all Men of Prudence and Industry, to whom its Attainment is an object of Ambition." And he never abandoned his opposition to the Repeal of the Corn Laws. His proposal to open places of amusement and instruction on Sundays shows, considering the date at which it was made, a foresight that is as startling as it is creditable.

It is inevitable that in such a survey as he makes in *Plain or Ringlets* he should show his limitations as well as his merits, and the thing that strikes us most forcibly once more is the smallness of his world. As ever he is concerned wholly with his own class and particularly with his own section of it which lived in the country. He knew the life of the towns, London and Brighton especially, but only as they affected the visitor from the country. Dickens, a cockney born and bred, knew his London by day and by night as few people since Dr. Samuel Johnson had ever known it. Thackeray knew the London of the clubs and the drawing-rooms and the shabby-genteel life of the lower middle-class. But to Surtees it was a place to which the country gentlemen came for amusements, for refreshment and for mental stimulation. And so he examines and approves London just in so far as it contributes to these ends. For if ever an English novelist had his roots firmly planted in the country it was Robert Smith Surtees—even more firmly than his great contemporary, Trollope. Thackeray was Anglo-Indian by tradition, urban by later upbringing and life. On his own confession, when he had to describe a hunting scene, he stole from Mr. Jorrocks. And of Dickens' world Sir Arthur Quiller-Couch writes, "Yes, this world is of the streets: in which Dickens was bred and from which he drew the miseries and consolations of his boyhood. A world 'full of folk,' but not, like Piers Plowman's, a 'field full of folk.' His understanding of England is in many ways as deep as Shakespeare's, but it is all, or almost all, of the urban England which in his day had already begun to kill the rural."

" You will remember," he adds later in the same lecture, " that *Pickwick* in its first conception was to deal with the adventures and misadventures of a sporting club after the fashion of the ' Handley Cross ' series by Surtees. . . . Now Surtees—not a great writer, but to this day (at any rate to me) a most amusing one—was, although like Dickens condemned to London and the Law, a north-country sportsman, and could ride and, it is reported, without riding for effect usually saw a deal of what the hounds were doing. The Pickwickian sportsmen had to decline *that* competition very soon!" " Shakespeare," he says again, " knew his London, his Eastcheap, its taverns. But when you think of Shakespeare, you think (I will challenge you) rather of rural England, of Avon, or Arden, of native wood notes wild." In the same way Surtees knew his London, his Brighton, his Boulogne, but when you think of him you think of Hamsterley and the north-country moors, of the drumming of hooves on turf, of the sound of a horn on a misty November morning. As a countryman—more experienced, more intellectually alive than most of his fellows, but none the less a countryman first and last—he was subject to a countryman's limitations.

Surtees' world, it must be admitted, was a small and an enclosed one, but he knew it perfectly. It is not until, as in *Plain or Ringlets* he leaves it for a little while and gazes at the larger world, that we realize how enclosed it was. For his larger world does not extend very far beyond the wall of the country gentleman's park, nor does he stray very far from the railway line that leads from the counties to London. Uneven as the book is, it has its value for that picture of the Victorian world and still more for the picture of man who looks at it. For once he has left the hunting field and walked abroad. " And no man," says the late Sir Walter Raleigh, " walks abroad save on his own shadow."

CHAPTER VII

The Ride Home

"I am now about, my friend, to take leave of you; and, at the same time that I give repose to you, let me entreat you to show the same favour to your hounds and horses."—PETER BECKFORD.

"There was a man wrote a book, and amongst other intelligent things he put in, was an observation that one cannot do an act not in itself morally evil for the last time without feelin's of regret: and if that be true with regard to indifferent things, 'ow much more tellin' must it be when applied to what may be called the liver and bacon of one's existence! To that noblest, sublimest, grandest, best of all sports, the gallant, cheerin' soul-stirrin' chass."—*Handley Cross.*

I

ROBERT SURTEES was writing his last novel, *Mr. Facey Romford's Hounds*, in the year 1862 and 1863, when he was nearly fifty-eight and within a year of his death. As the thoughts of ageing men will, his were turning back towards his vanished youth. He had made his experiment in *Plain or Ringlets* and he would experiment no more. He had walked abroad, but the hunting field recalled him and—how joyfully we can only imagine—he left the world of picnic, regatta and flirtation for the world that he really knew and understood. *Mr. Facey Romford's Hounds* takes us back twelve years and plunges us back again into the world of *Mr. Sponge's Sporting Tour*. It might almost be a sequel to *Mr. Sponge*, so much does it resemble it in character, in incident and in setting. Nearly all of the characters have appeared in the earlier work—Mr. Romford himself, Lucy Glitters, Soapey Sponge, Robert Foozle. But Surtees' memories go back beyond that to the Reverend James Birkett of Ovingham School, the maker of gibbey-sticks, who appeared first in *Mr. Sponge* and now reappears in *Facey Romford*: to the hunting days with the London packs when he learned to despise the hunting of the carted deer, a hatred which he perpetuates in Mr. Stotford and the run with the Benicia Boy: and even to Hamsterley itself, with its hunting and that vision that he always kept before him of Mr. Ralph Lambton as the perfect master. It is as though in his last book he is gathering up the threads of all his bygone experience and presenting them in a final piece of work, knitted together and complete. Neither Surtees nor Leech lived to see the book published, for both died in 1864 and *Mr. Romford* was published by Bradbury and Evans in monthly parts starting in May 1864, two months after Surtees' death, and in one volume in 1865. There were to have been twenty-four coloured plates by Leech, but he died after having done fourteen of them and the remaining ten were provided by Hablot K. Browne. Phiz had illustrated Surtees' first novel, *Jorrocks's Jaunts and Jollities*, in 1838 and *Hawbuck Grange* in 1847. It was fitting that he should have survived to complete the series with the last ten plates for *Mr. Facey Romford's Hounds*.

In every way *Facey Romford* is a return to an earlier manner. There is nothing in it of the uncertainty of *Plain or Ringlets* or the patchwork of *Ask Mamma*. It might have followed directly upon *Mr. Sponge's Sporting Tour* without the twelve years' interval that actually separates them. It is a straightforward sporting novel, a hunting comedy as lively, as amusing and as competent as anything he ever wrote. It is satirical but less bitter in its satire than any work since *Young Tom Hall*. Surtees cannot leave his old enemies, the domestic servants, alone ; and *Facey Romford* provides us with Swig and Chowey, the hunt servants who were reasonably competent if they could be kept away from the gin bottle, and with " Mrs. Mustard's miscellany," Dirty No. 1, Dirty No. 2, Dirty No. 3, and Dirtiest of the Dirty. But there is a welcome absence of the hunting aristocrats and of the soldiers. The satire is mostly directed at the new rich, Mr. and Mrs. Watkins, Mr. Hazey and his boy Bill, " Ten-and-a-half-per-cent " and " Five-thousand-a-year "—at all that class of successful tradesmen who were spreading over the country and beginning to infest the hunting field. But the sport is too serious for over much satire.

There is nothing wrong with Mr. Facey Romford's pack except the method by which he acquired them. It was his great good fortune constantly to be mistaken for the " other " Mr. Facey Romford of Abbey-field Pack, a mistake which he did nothing to correct. By using that gentleman's name, credit and seal, " A Turbot sitting upon its tail on a cap of Dignity," Facey was able to provide himself at no personal expense with drafts from the Belvoir, the Beaufort, the Bramham and other first-rate packs. By the same method he amassed saddlery, clothes and every sort of hunting equipment, and as a final triumph got Beldon Hall, the property of Lord Lovetin, who had been at Eton with the other Mr. Romford. There is a tense scene towards the end of the book,

Facey Romford treats Sponge to a little music

[MR. SPONGE'S SPORTING TOUR]

just before the final exposure of Mr. Romford and Lucy Glitters, when Lord Lovetin, who had grown suspicious, arrived, unexpected and unannounced, at Beldon Hall. " His Lordship started, for he thought to give his old schoolfellow an agreeable surprise ; and Romford started, for he was not accustomed to intruders, and didn't want to be troubled. They then stood staring at one another like Spanish pointers, each wondering who the other was.

" Lord Lovetin at length broke silence. ' Beg pardon,' said he, ' but I thought it was Mr. Romford.'

" ' Romford it is,' said Facey, yawning, and stretching out his great arms as if to show the intruder what he had to contend with.

" ' But not the Romford I was at school with,' observed his Lordship, eyeing him intently.

" ' Don't know who you are, to begin with,' replied Facey ; ' but moy name's Romford,' observed he ; ' *that oi'll swear to*.'

" ' I'm Lord Lovetin,' replied his Lordship mildly."

It was the end of Mr. Romford just as the Countess of Caperington's snub was the end of Lucy Glitters. But Surtees, as we have remarked before, could never bear to deal out final punishment. So like the Micawber family they all end happily in the Antipodes—Facey with his wife Cassandra Cleopatra and the twins, and Lucy reunited to Mr. Sponge, who had gone out there some years earlier still owing Mr. Romford the seven pounds ten, which he lost to him at cards in the *Sporting Tour* some twelve years before.

" The last account heard of Soapey and him was that they were going to set up a bank in Collins Street East, under the firm of

' ROMFORD AND SPONGE '

" Good luck attend their exertions, say we ! We expect to hear of their setting up a pack of hounds together next."

Mr. Sponge disappears early in the book, but Lucy Glitters remains to the end, and she improves on acquaintance. She still rides to hounds, whips-in to Mr. Romford, and shows off horses for sale, but in *Facey Romford's Hounds* she emerges more as a person than as a female horse-coper. She passes herself off as Mr. Romford's sister or sister-in-law—the exact relationship is not clear nor is it meant to be—and with her mother in attendance she settles down to keep house for him at Beldon Hall. Dubious as her methods are, it is impossible not to admire her courage and resource. She had been an actress, and she understood dress and

"Most pernicious woman!"

décor: with the aid of her friend Betsy Shannon, also of the profession, and of a complacent theatrical costumier she makes a presentable domestic staff out of the Dirties, Billy Balsam and Bob Short. And as leading lady she is superb until her final exposure by the Countess of Caperington, who had been Lady Scattercash and before that Miss Spangles of the Theatre Royal, Bungington. Lucy had many faults, but she never forgot or turned from an old friend, and her rejection by this old friend is the more painful. Surtees seldom attempted pathos, and when he did he was generally, as at the death of Jack Spraggon, at a loss. But there is something genuinely pathetic in this scene—in the countess's cold stare, Romford's stricken silence, the startled glances of the field, and the sobbing, dejected figure of Lucy, riding slowly away on Leotard who had been the cause of all the trouble. For he had been sold to the countess, whom he threw off over his tail.

Yet the exposure was long overdue, and they had had an astonishingly long run for nearly everybody else's money. Together they were a formidable couple: they could have given even Colonel and Mrs. Rawdon Crawley some hints on how to live on nothing a year. And if Lucy acquired her belongings dishonestly she was no niggard with them: she clothed her mother handsomely and entertained her old friend of the profession, Betsy Shannon, in the most generous way. And her management of Mr. Romford, who cared for nothing but hunting, was masterly. She made him dress properly and took him out to dinner, and eventually by a miracle of tact and diplomacy she got him to consent to her giving a reception and dance at Beldon Hall. Facey was not sociably inclined. His idea of high living was "Sheep-chops," batter pudding and gin. He strongly objected to being taken out to dinner. "He didn't feel comfortable out," he said. "He hadn't a dress coat. The women bothered him. He didn't know what to say to them. He didn't know how to get them in to dinner. He didn't know how to get them out again." And he dreaded speech-making, which was one of the inevitable duties of a master of hounds, though, when he couldn't avoid it, he went at it as he would at a fence. "Gentlemen, I'm no speaker, but I'm a sportsman. If you'll let my hounds alone, and give them fair play and room to hunt, I'll be bound to say I'll show you sport, but if you override them—I—I—don't know what I'll do. S'pose then that we drink 'Foxhunting' and be off to it!" It was his maiden speech, delivered at Mr. Joseph Large's hunt breakfast, and after all it covers everything that need be said.

III

"It will be the last serial that I shall attempt," Surtees wrote to John Leech of *Mr. Facey Romford's Hounds.* His mind during the last years of his life was turning from fiction to autobiography and he was contemplating a book of memoirs to be called "Sporting and Social Recollections." Mr. E. D. Cuming, in his *Robert Smith Surtees, Creator of 'Jorrocks'* explains that by an oversight the drafts for this work were filed away with the notes that Surtees had made on his work as Justice of the Peace, and it was not realized till many years later that they were in fact the first sketches for his memoirs. He also records the very important fact that there is a note among the Hamsterley papers that the "Sporting and Social Recollections" were to be published under their author's name. So the anonymity of a lifetime was to be abandoned, and for the first time since 1831 a book was to come out bearing the name of R. S. Surtees. It would seem that Surtees considered it proper to set his name to a technical work like *The Horseman's Manual* or to a volume of reminiscences, though not to works of fiction. But the "Sporting and Social Recollections" had never progressed beyond the very earliest stages. Mr. Cuming edited a selection of them in 1923. "Some of these rough drafts," he writes, "must have been lost. It is evident that Surtees had written something relating to his early life: the opening sentence of his account of Mr. Birkett's school clearly indicates that this continues a record. All the MSS. are incomplete: numerous sheets bear nothing save a few words, which manifestly were to serve as reminders or 'key-notes': others break off abruptly, the sentence unfinished: in others again are blanks, left until the writer's memory should enable him to fill in place-names, proper names or dates." Before he could settle down to these memoirs, Surtees was anxious to get Mr. Romford safely launched and out of the way, but the task proved to be unusually difficult. In the summer of 1861 he had got far enough with the manuscript to approach Bradbury and Evans about its publication in serial form with Leech's illustrations. The publishers were more than glad to have it, but suggested deferring publication till the following year in order to give Leech plenty of time to do his part and to ensure that—as was not always the case when he was concerned—the illustrations should be forthcoming just when they were needed. But, as usual, time was just what Leech lacked. In addition to all his ordinary work he was engaged in illustrating *Mr. Punch's Almanac* and was also preparing that strange exhibition of his own oil-paintings that was to startle the artistic world of 1863. It was a departure from the practice of a life-time, for he had always thought little of the practice of painting in oils, deriding the time that it wasted and the trouble that it involved in detail and finish. "I am not credited for oil-painting," he said, "I should never have the patience for it." And he added the remarkable comment that "Finish, in my opinion, is a waste of time" —remarkable indeed when one considers the exquisite detail and finish of his pen drawings and coloured prints.

But some strange impulse drove him at the age of forty-five to embark on a new career, and his method was as strange as the impulse. He chose a number of his *Punch* drawings, enlarged them on to canvas and covered them with a thin wash of oil-paint. This collection he exhibited in a London gallery, and even his biographer and wholesale admirer, Mr. W.P. Frith, R.A., can find little good to say of them. Yet the venture met with more success than could have been anticipated or even than it deserved and brought in to Leech a sum of nearly £5000. Leach had Thackeray to thank for this. Thackeray, who was always ready to do a good turn for a friend, wrote in *The Times* an enthusiastic notice of the exhibition which does more credit to his loyalty than to his artistic taste or knowledge, but which did undoubtedly attract public interest. Thackeray died only a few months later and Surtees, who had always been friendly with him, felt his loss deeply. They had not met very often during the last few years, for Surtees was mostly at Hamsterley and Thackeray was busy with the editorship of the *Cornhill Magazine*. "I was much shocked at the death of poor Thackeray," Surtees wrote to Leech, "to my mind by far the foremost writer of the age. I always thought him ailing and had not seen much of him since he took the *Cornhill*, conceiving that he had plenty to do without being troubled with his country acquaintances. I hope he has left his family in comfortable circumstances. They deserve to be, I'm sure, for there never was a better fellow."

Leech, replying in the letter in which he expressed his hope of "putting on the red coat again" with Surtees and Facey Romford, wrote, "You are right about poor dear Thackeray. He was one of my oldest and best friends and his loss to me is a loss indeed." Thackeray, Leech and Surtees had always been good friends and within the next ten months all three of them were to die. Thackeray at the age of 52, Leech at 47 and Surtees at nearly 60. They were all over six feet high—an unimportant point, but it is the sort of thing that binds men together. And they had many things in common—they came from the same class and knew the same world, the London clubs and the big country houses. Thackeray was no sportsman, but both Leech and Surtees hunted, and Leech and Thackeray had a common interest in art and especially in draughtsmanship. Surtees was approaching that time of life when a man begins to see the friends of his youth and middle age drop off one by one. He had worked with Leech for many years and they had always been on the best of terms : cantankerous as he could be, he never quarrelled with John Leech in spite of delays and hindrances caused by Leech's excess of work and his occasionally dilatory ways. Perhaps their friendship owes much to Leech's tact and readiness to subordinate the artist to the author, for there can never have been a pleasanter man to work with. Surtees appreciated and was as anxious as ever to have Leech's collaboration in what he insists is to be his last work of fiction.

> My Dear Leech [he writes in 1864]
>
> Greetings. Do you think there is any chance of our getting together again in the way of work ? I was in hopes *Romford* would have made his appearance next month, but as yet I have no prelude in the shape of a prospectus. I should much like if we could finish together. How say you, John Leech, shall it be a go or not ?

It was Surtees' last appeal to Leech and it was successful, for Leech replied offering to start the illustrations in February or March at the latest. It was a relief to Surtees, who had seriously feared the year before that Leech had taken permanently to oil-painting and was about to give up illustrating. So strong was this fear that he actually got as far as offering *Facey Romford* to *The Field* as a serial story without illustrations. But *The Field* had no room for it at the moment and fortunately Leech had not taken permanently to oil-painting. His somewhat odd exhibition had satisfied the craving and provided him with some welcome cash. By March 1864 the whole text of *Facey Romford* was complete, but as it was to come out in monthly parts there was still time for Leech to illustrate it, and under pressure he produced the two plates for the first number. Bradbury and Evans published the first number in May, but two months before its appearance Surtees had died suddenly at Brighton. Leech continued to illustrate it till October, on the 29th day of which month he, too, died; and Hablot K. Browne (Phiz) finished the work.

IV

Though Surtees in 1863 and 1864 was harping on the fact that *Facey Romford* was to be his last work of fiction, it is not to be thought that he had any presentiment that it was to be his last work of any sort. He was preparing the "Sporting and Social Recollections" and there was no reason to think that his health was precarious or that his physical or mental vigour was failing. He still hunted regularly, though his nerve was not as good as it had been and he was not riding as close to hounds as had been his custom. But he had never been especially robust, as so many of the Surtees men were not, and later in life he suffered from the bitter cold of the northern winters. In severe weather, when it seemed likely that frost would confine hounds to kennel for some time, he began to take the opportunity of seeking a warmer climate and with Mrs. Surtees he used to visit Brighton, staying usually at Mutton's Hotel. But he seemed as vigorous as ever and was still ready for a fight if he thought that injustice was being done to him or anyone for whom he felt responsible. In 1859 and 1860 he was at war with the Poor Law Guardians over the case of an old cottager called Athey, who had applied for and been granted Poor Law Relief. Surtees had supported the application and was highly indignant when the guardians cancelled the grant on discovering that Athey possessed two cows. Anything that savoured of injustice instantly aroused Surtees and he not only wrote to the Guardians in protest, but rode over from Hamsterley to attend their meeting and to insist on justice for Athey. Always a spirited opponent, he carried the war into their own country, for, finding out that the Guardians were taking pay for their services, he wrote to the Poor Law Board in London, questioning the legality of the proceedings. The Board's reply has not been preserved, but apparently the local Guardians were overcome by his attack, and Athey kept his relief and his cows. The whole episode is typical of Surtees, of his sense of responsibility, his pugnacity and his love of justice. And a few years later, just before his death, he had his last struggle with the railway promoters—over a projected branch of the Derwent Valley line from Newcastle to Consett which was to involve the building of a viaduct to span the Pont Valley within half a mile of Hamsterley Hall. As we have seen over and over again in his novels he appreciated the benefits—the " great, the crowning benefits " he calls them—that the railways had brought with them. But admiration of abstract benefits is one thing and toleration of a viaduct within half a mile of Hamsterley is another. His opposition was so determined that the promoters of the line deferred to him to some extent and produced an alternative scheme which pleased him no better. " I don't want the railway," he wrote, " which cuts me most desperately to waste." He took advice from his lawyers, who wished him to bow to the inevitable and pointed out what an advantage to his coal interests the new line would be. Like any sensible man he could appreciate the value of anything that improved his assets. But no asset could weigh with him against the violation of Hamsterley. He maintained his opposition, but in 1862 the Bill for promoting the railway passed through Parliament, though the contract for the building of the viaduct was not signed until four months after his death. The late winter of 1864 was a hard one and the frost persisted into March. It was plain that there could be no hunting for some time; so, as was their custom, Mr. and Mrs. Surtees left Hamsterley for Brighton. They stayed at Mutton's Hotel in the King's Road and Surtees appeared to be in his usual health. On the night of the sixteenth he went to bed at the usual time, but awoke during the night and complained of pain in the region of his heart. He died within ten minutes. His body was taken back to Hamsterley Hall and buried in Ebchester Churchyard.

It is said of Thackeray that once, on picking up the biography of an author, he remarked, " I hope there will be none of this damned nonsense about me when I am dead." His wishes were scrupulously respected by his family, and even to-day no authentic and full-length biography exists. It is easy to imagine Surtees, who was Thackeray's friend, saying the same thing, for they had many tastes in common and not least a hatred of display and a habit of decent reticence. Nor, it must be admitted, was it a life so abounding in incident or romance as to attract the biographer in search of a story : still less was it touched with scandal so as to attract the biographer in search of sensation. It is the story of a country gentleman and sportsman, more erudite and articulate than most of his fellows : devoted to his family and his estate, serious and knowledgeable about his sport : austere in private life but no Puritan : a loyal and generous friend, a resolute but not implacable enemy :

honest and courteous, conscious of his own importance and ready to defend it, but never to assert it: prudent in money matters, hating extravagance and empty show. Apart from his writing, it is a life such as thousands of country gentlemen have lived. Even so, the brief paragraphs allotted to him in the *Dictionary of National Biography* in 1892, the first published work to give any account of his life, are pitifully inadequate. It was in any case a mistake to allot the writing of them to Thomas Seccombe, who knew little of country life, and less of sport. It might be suspected, too, that he knew little of Surtees' books, for he plainly confused *Handley Cross* with *Hillingdon Hall* when he wrote, "*Handley Cross*, in which Jorrocks reappears as a Master of Fox Hounds and the possessor of a Country seat." His mention of the "coarseness of the text" suggests that he adopted, without sufficient thought, the attitude of Surtees' contemporaries. In fact the only thing to be said in Seccombe's favour is that it compares favourably with Austin Dobson's article in the same publication on John Leech in which he refers to Robert *Scott* Surtees. It is, one would have thought, not only an elementary requirement of biography, but a common courtesy to get a proper name correct, but the present generation has not improved on Austin Dobson, for Dame Una Pope-Hennessey's *Charles Dickens*, published in 1947 mentions *Richard* Smith Surtees.

No attempt to write his life was made until 1923 when Mr. E. D. Cuming, having had access to the private papers at Hamsterley, published a selection of them with an illuminating preface and commentary, under the name of *Robert Smith Surtees, Creator of 'Jorrocks,'* 1803–1864. It is not, and does not, profess to be a coherent biography, still less a critical study, but it is an important book, the first serious contribution to Surtees literature, and one which no student of Surtees can afford to neglect. It was followed ten years later by Mr. Frederick Watson's *Robert Smith Surtees*, a critical study which deals with his novels and characters and with his importance as a social historian. It contains, too, some most valuable chapters on his reaction upon his contemporaries and on the modern mind. But apart from these works and a few admirable articles in *Blackwood's Magazine*, mainly by Mr. E. D. Cuming and Miss Moira O'Neill, there has been little enough published about his life. All of his great contemporaries—with the single exception of Thackeray—have fared better, or at least more generously, at the hands of biographers.

V

When we turn from the biographers to the critics, we find that he has received hardly more generous treatment. There are scores of historical and critical books on Victorian literature in which he is not mentioned at all ; and all too often when he is mentioned it is in a tone of something like patronage. He appeared—most unjustly, we feel—to his contemporaries and his immediate successors as a gross, cynically jesting figure, scoffing at the purer virtues and the gentler graces. It was a serious age and one not a little pompous, and it had no use for Robert Surtees, who was seldom serious, never pompous and most emphatically never pretentious.

The twentieth-century critics began to see him in a truer perspective, and such serious and excellent critics as Sir Arthur Quiller-Couch, Professor George Saintsbury and Mrs. Virginia Woolf have all found him worthy of notice among the writers of English fiction. Sir Arthur's opinion has already been quoted, " not a great writer, but to me, to this day, a very amusing one." Professor Saintsbury concurs in his book *The English Novel* when he calls him " Nearly always readable and sometimes very amusing, even to those who are not exactly Nimrods." And in his *Nineteenth Century Literature* he allows him " much knowledge and not inconsiderable wit." Few men have known more about the English language and its literature than Professor Saintsbury, but it is a little surprising to find him, in *The English Novel*, comparing Surtees unfavourably with Charles Kingsley. Writing of Kingsley's *Yeast*, he says, " It is curious to compare this (dealing largely as it does with sport) and the Jorrocks series of Robert Smith Surtees. Kingsley was nearly as practical a sportsman as Surtees, but Surtees' characters and manners have the old artificial-picaresque quality."

Mr. Ernest A. Baker in his *History of the English Novel* makes a fair summing-up of Surtees' virtues and failings and is perhaps the first critic to appreciate his value as a social historian and the fact that what really underlies his satire is a hatred of sham and pretentiousness. He is not quite accurate in describing Surtees as " a briefless barrister " and a little less than fair in saying that he had " no imagination." But apart from these blemishes his opinion is fair and favourable, and he is also the first critic to appreciate at his true worth that immortal figure whom an earlier generation had written off as a coarse cockney grocer. " Jorrocks," he writes, " makes the world laugh, but it is not as a butt ; he is the mouthpiece with his Sancho, James Pigg, of his master's scorn."

Of the novels as a whole he writes, " It might almost be said that his characters are composed of nothing but manners and mannerisms," but that the books, " apart from their interest to the sportsman, constitute a great page of social history and contain a world of shrewd comment and broad satire on John Bull's foibles and eccentricities." And he concludes, " Surtees wore his cantankerousness, his annoyance at shams, his indignation at absurdities on his sleeve ; and a transparent honesty shines through the boisterous and aggressive laughter." There have been few better comments.

One of the most remarkable tributes comes from Mrs. Woolf in her *Common Reader*—remarkable because Mrs. Woolf had no great affinity with or sympathy for hunting men, and because, while few critics have appreciated or even noticed Surtees as a stylist, the tribute comes from the most unquestionable stylist of our generation. " Indeed," Mrs. Woolf wrote, " the English Sporting writers, Beckford, St. John, Surtees, Nimrod make no mean reading. In their slapdash, gentlemanly way they have ridden their pens as boldly as they have ridden their horses. They have had their effect upon the language. This riding and tumbling, this being blown upon and rained upon and splashed from head to heels with mud, have worked themselves into the very texture of English Prose and given it that leap and dash, that stripping of images from flying hedge and tossing tree which distinguishes it not indeed above the French but so emphatically from it."

Mr. Harold Child, writing in the *Cambridge History of English Literature*, is afflicted by the chronic inaccuracy that prevails about Surtees as a man, when he calls him the son of " a Yorkshire landowner." But of Surtees the author he has deep understanding and almost unqualified approval. " It is possible," he writes, " that the true worth of Surtees' work has been a little obscured by the fame of the author of Pickwick, of which the original idea, a tale of cockney sporting life, was to some extent suggested by the adventures of Mr. Jorrocks. Surtees is a comic writer of a broad and hearty humour and a deft and subtle touch. In the invention of comic character and speech he comes second only to Dickens. Mr. Jorrocks, Facey Romford, Lord Scamperdale and his friend Jack Spraggon, Mr. Sponge, Mr. Jawleyford of Jawleyford Court—these with nearly every character that Surtees troubles to elaborate are rich in humour, while the dialogue in these novels has a force and flavour comparable only with that of Dickens, or in some piece of flourishing invective in Nash or Greene. Surtees' comedy is, doubtless, like that of Dickens mainly a comedy of humorous or personal oddities: and Surtees it must be admitted was careless about construction and about such necessary ingredients of a novel as did not interest him: but all the fun is rooted in human nature and set out with abounding energy."

It is hardly possible to quarrel with the unanimous verdict of these authorities, a verdict which is best summed up in Quiller-Couch's "not a great, but to this day a very amusing writer." It would be idle to assert that he is great in the sense that Shakespeare or Dickens are great, men whose work is based on a universal knowledge of and sympathy with mankind. Nor had he that intellectual greatness which we find in George Eliot nor the perfection of form of Jane Austen or Thackeray.

But if we must admit that he was not great in comparison with his fellow Victorians as a whole, we can hardly deny that in his own line, the sporting novel, he towered above the other writers of his time. The middle of the nineteenth century saw the death of the English sporting novel, as England turned from the fields to the towns. Since that time the sporting—especially the hunting—novel has only reappeared spasmodically and then usually in the hands of Irish writers. In Surtees' days there was a flourishing school of sporting novelists and it is the measure of how near he came to greatness to compare him with the rest of them. Nimrod, of whom J. G. Lockhart said that he "could hunt like Hugo Meynell and write like Walter Scott," is a lively and knowledgeable writer, ruined by flamboyance and snobbery, and to-day only survives as a curiosity. Charles Kingsley "nearly as practical a sportsman as Surtees," in Saintsbury's phrase, had always his evangelical axe to grind. Whyte-Melville, as accomplished a horseman as a writer, while he could describe a hunt as well as any man who ever wrote, never created a character that remains in the memory. F. E. Smedley wrote several amusing novels that are almost unknown to-day. In their time they all enjoyed a measure of success, but of all that school only Surtees survives because only he left a permanent addition to the stock of English characters. It is unhappily true that all that most people to-day know of Surtees is the name "Jorrocks." Yet that is something. Who to-day remembers Lancelot Smith, Tilbury Nogo or Francis Raby?

He survives too, deservedly, as a social historian—"a great page of social history," Mr. Ernest Baker says of him. It may have been a small world that he knew, but he described it with such accuracy and such wealth of detail, above all with such knowledge and understanding, that it forms an imperishable record. And if it was small it was not unimportant. In his time England was still an agricultural country and even to-day agriculture is its chief industry. Country gardens, suburban plots and town allotments all bear witness to the fact that Englishmen have not yet forgotten their traditional occupation of wresting food and beauty from the soil. Agriculture in this country has been much at the mercy of politicians who have neglected and upheld it spasmodically according to their fleeting necessities. They have treated it much as the public have treated the fighting services, as a shield and bulwark in time of war, a jest and extravagance in time of peace. But agriculture and sport—the two things of which Surtees wrote—are very close to the heart of England and his absorption in them makes Surtees a peculiarly English writer.

Mrs. Virginia Woolf has testified that he and his fellow sportsmen have left their mark on English style. It is well they did so and more than well that it was just at that time, for a corrective was needed or soon would be. Whatever the late Victorians contributed to the English novel—and it is impossible to exaggerate the importance of their contribution—their effect on its style was not wholly to its advantage. Too often the writing became heavy, the tone didactic, the sentimentality cloying. Far too often, under the disguise of the novel, lurked the tract and the sermon. The broad jollity of *Handley Cross*, the astringency of Soapey Sponge and Facey Romford were needed to preserve the balance, to enable a later generation to be profound without being portentous and to present psychology without losing all sight of humour. And humour is the greatest legacy which Surtees left to the English novel.

VI

In his *Art of Writing* Sir A. T. Quiller-Couch lays down four requirements for a good English style. It must, he says, be accurate, perspicuous, persuasive and appropriate: and measured by these standards Surtees may fairly lay claim to be a stylist of high order. If he fails at all it is in accuracy—that is in precision of grammar and nicety in the use of words. Mrs. Woolf calls his style "Gentlemanly and slapdash" and there can hardly be a better description. He was certainly careless in construction and more than a little slipshod in his diction in those parts of the book which obviously interested him least. His gravest fault in style is a habit of using over and over again a cliché, either borrowed or of his own invention, and an occasional facetious turn of phrase which seems to come from habit rather than from thought. Someone in his youth must have told him about the sailor who said that he had had " beef, mutton and cheese—all the delicacies of the season " and this not very amusing conceit appears in all the books and more than once in several of them. His use of the catch-phrase, " we beg pardon," is even more frequent and quite as irritating. He writes of " Lucy Glitters —we beg pardon Mrs. Somerville," or " the kind of man—we beg pardon gentleman," as often as he uses his other favourite catch-phrase, " the order of the day." " Munch, crunch, munch was then the order of the day," is his usual descriptive phrase for a dinner or a hunt-breakfast and " Jog, jog, bump, bump, trot trot, was then the order of the day," serves for the field moving off from the meet.

He has, too, a persistent habit of describing any noise made by a man or an animal by an onomatopoeic word and repeating the word as often as the noise occurs and as long as it sounds. Horns always go " toot-toot," cats " mew-mew," and the wind " shoosh." And no character in the book can sneeze, cough, hiccup, smoke or make any kind of noise without its being painstakingly recorded. It is his most persistent and most wearisome habit, but scarcely less persistent is his fondness for calling his characters by names that personify their leading qualities—Sir Harry Scattercash, Mr. Bottleends the butler, Mr. Fleeceall the lawyer and their fellows. But it was the convention of the time and he adopted it—and having adopted it, rode it to death as he was apt to ride his conceits. He carried it to far greater lengths than did his contemporaries though they nearly all indulged in the same practice. Dickens had Lord Frederick Verisopht and Sir Mulberry Hawk, Mr. Pyke and Mr. Pluck as well as the less famous Mrs. Wrymug and Mr. Gallanbile. Disraeli had the mill owners Shuffle and Screw, Trollope had the Reverend Mr. Quiverful, Charles Kingsley had Mrs. Newbroom, Lord Vieuxbois and the Reverend Panurgus Blazeaway. And even Thackeray, the most fastidious of writers, adorned Mrs. Rawdon Crawley's evening party with the Dowager Duchess of Stilton, the Duc de le Gruyère, Marchioness of Cheshire, Comte de Brie and several other aristocratic cheeses. So it would be unfair to blame Surtees unduly for Mrs. Rowley Rounding and Sir Archibald Depecarde.

Laboured and verbose as his descriptions are, there is no excuse for any reader of Surtees not knowing exactly what his characters looked like, or how they dressed. His description of clothing are as accurate and detailed as his descriptions of persons. And his persuasiveness, his ability to make his readers see with his own eyes, is never more in evidence than when hounds are running. Nimrod and Whyte-Melville can express the thrill of the run from the horseman's point of view, the yawning ditches, the towering hedges, but on anyone except a horseman they soon begin to pall. It is all a little too dashing, too extravagant, but what takes the interest from it is the fact that the people who are riding are not of any consequence. The gallop is the thing: the characters are only there because the horses must have men on their backs.

No higher tribute can be paid to Surtees' persuasiveness than the fact that his hunting runs can be and are read with enjoyment by men who have never ridden to hounds nor even laid leg across a horse. Such runs as those with the Goose and Dumpling Hounds in *Hawbuck Grange*, the " Cat and Custard-Pot " day in *Handley Cross*, or the Calderlaw Common run with Mr. Facey Romford and the Heavyside Hunt are first-rate pieces of descriptive writing. To the hunting man there is the interest of seeing hounds work, the check and the cast, the final run into view. To the horseman there is the varied delight in the performance of the different horses, the chances of rail and water—a slower more detailed description than the whirlwind steeplechases of Nimrod and Whyte-Melville. But for the great mass of us who are neither hunting men nor horsemen there is the outstanding attraction of the fact that never throughout the run does Surtees lose sight of the men who follow the hounds.

It is noticeable, too, how his style alters when hounds are running, to match the speed and rhythm of the hunt. It becomes crisper and terser, the dialogue is in curt sentences, jerked out by breathless and excited men. Diffuse and verbose as he sometimes is in the less active parts of his writing, he prunes it of all but the barest necessities when the action calls for it. His style is in fact in the fullest sense what Quiller-Couch calls " appropriate." In the inn and the dining-room he is long-winded enough. But when the hounds break out of cover he rides his pen, in Mrs. Woolf's phrase, as gallantly as he rode his horse. " Slapdash and gentlemanly " she calls his style: and hunting is after all a slapdash and gentlemanly occupation.

VII

The real strength of Surtees' style is in his dialogue and it is not too much to say that in this department of his art he surpassed his great contemporaries by as much as he came short of them in other ways. The great Victorians, with all their merits, were as a rule indifferent writers of dialogue. They seemed to ignore the fundamental fact that men and women in ordinary conversation do not talk coherent prose. Their characters could hardly say good-morning to each other without making a speech about it. "'How do you do, Adam, Bede?' said Dinah Morris. 'I trust you feel rested and strengthened again to bear the burthen and heat of the day.'" Dinah Morris, to be sure, was a preacher, but even so the style is over-laboured for the triviality of the occasion. And Major Dobbin and Amelia Osborne are hardly less portentous when they discuss the piano which he had given her.

"'I was very ungrateful,' Amelia said.

"'No: only indifferent,' Dobbin continued desperately, 'I have nothing to make a woman otherwise. I know what you are feeling now. You are hurt in your heart at the discovery about the piano: and that it came from me and not from George. I forgot, or I should not have spoken of it so. It is for me to ask your pardon for being a fool for a moment and thinking that years of constancy and devotion might have pleaded with you.'

"'It is you who are cruel now,' Amelia said with some spirit. 'George is my husband, here and in heaven. How could I love any other but him? I am his as when you first saw me, dear William. It was he who told me how good and generous you were and who taught me to love you as a brother. Have you not been everything to me and my boy? Our dearest, truest, kindest friend and protector? Had you come a few months sooner perhaps you might have spared me that—that dreadful parting. It nearly killed me, William—but you didn't come, though I wished and prayed for you to come, and they took him, too, away from me. Isn't he a noble boy, William? Be his friend still, and mine.'"

It may be pleaded that both William and Amelia were labouring under strong emotion. Yet it is a fact—though the Victorians seemed to be unaware of it—that the higher or stronger the emotion, the less coherent and grammatical is its expression. The sincerest talk of lovers consists only too often of broken phrases and repeated clichés: and anyone who has suffered a severe shock or a sudden and deep grief knows how readily the heart finds expression in the most trivial and conventional phrases. There are few stronger emotions than the generous anger that is aroused by the sight of wanton cruelty. But in real life the over-wrought spirit generally vents itself in spluttered oaths and broken, ungrammatical phrases and not in such fluent prose as sprang to Nicholas Nickleby's lips when he saw Mr. Squeers thrashing Smike.

Mr. Squeers's part of the dialogue rings true, being brief, furious and insulting. His "Sit down, beggar!" is true to type, conveying as it does the worst insult that he could think of on the spur of the moment. But it is hard to believe that any young man in the grip of a powerful emotion could spontaneously turn such phrases as "my indignation is aggravated by the dastardly cruelties practised on helpless infancy in this foul den." It has too much the air of a carefully prepared speech, just as have those elaborate objurgations of Jack Spraggon's which are too perfect to be genuine. But there was some excuse for Jack, who was maintained by Lord Scamperdale to do his cursing for him and who may wisely have enlarged the vocabulary and polished the phrases with which he earned his living. Nicholas sprang up in fury on an impulse: an occasion when most men splutter, stammer, turn brick-red and swear meaninglessly. The finest and most literary philippics are prepared in the study and let off in public after due calculation. There is something far more spontaneous and genuine in Mr. Jorrocks's "I'm much obliged to that gen'l'man with the big calves for over ridin' my 'ounds—werry much 'bliged to him, most 'ticklarly 'bliged to him! most confoundedly 'bliged to him! G-d-d-n 'bliged to him! Wish the devil had him, big calves and all."

But Surtees really did know how people talked. From the earliest discussion at the meet in the *Jaunts and Jollities* to the last talk in *Facey Romford* the books are crammed with dialogue of the very best sort—crisp, accurate, colloquial, amusing and above all natural. So many of the Victorians seem to have written not so much what their characters said as what they ought to have said. Their speech conveys their meaning clearly enough, but conveys it in the accents of the study, the lecture-room or the pulpit. They were hindered—as Surtees was never hindered—by the fact that the characters were bursting with the highest and most creditable of emotions and while their reactions to the emotions are true and in character their expression of them is at its worst nothing but *oratio obliqua* enclosed in inverted commas. Few of Surtees' characters were troubled by creditable emotions, but still fewer of them are guilty of falseness of expression. He was usually writing comic dialogue which does not lend itself to pomposity except for the purpose of mocking it.

When the higher emotions and virtues are not concerned there is much good dialogue in all the Victorians. Jos Sedley and Becky Sharp ; Pendennis and Warrington ; Mr. and Mrs. Poyser ; Sam Weller and his father ; the clergy of Barchester. The talk is always good as long as it remains between the two extremes of emotion and humour. The emotional talk is apt to lean towards pomposity and the humorous to exaggeration. In Dickens it is especially noticeable, and the comic dialogue, amusing as it always is, has an air of virtuosity ; it seems to be recorded less for its expression of the thoughts of the speakers than for its own sake. At its best it is superb, as it is when Sam Weller or Bob Sawyer are talking, because their wit is the typical wit of the cockney and the medical student. But Mrs. Wilfer, Mr. Mantalini, even Mr. Micawber begin to pall after a time—not as characters but as conversationalists. It would seem that a comic character in Dickens must be funny all the time whether he has anything to say or not. His duty in the book is to provide the comic relief and he provides it sometimes at the cost of being unbearably facetious.

There is no exaggeration in Surtees' dialogue, which is often at its best in the quieter passages. He is not obliged to force the comic relief since there is nothing in the books that needs relief, and so it follows that his characters are talking in their normal accents and at their normal level. There is no virtuosity in the dialogue itself. With the exception of Mr. Jorrocks, who was a humorist in word as well as in deed, there is hardly a character whose speech is worth quoting as purely humorous dialogue. It is too natural, too life-like. It is always the speech of characters, humorous in themselves, who have no need of verbal fireworks. A typical example is the conversation between Lord Scamperdale and Jack Spraggon after hunting on the day when Mr. Sponge first attracted Lord Scamperdale's unfavourable notice.

" 'Oh, Jack, I'm onhappy !' exclaimed he. 'I'm distressed !' continued he. 'I'm wretched !' added he, slapping his knees. 'I'm perfectly *miserable* !' he concluded, with a strong emphasis on the 'miserable.'

" 'What's the matter ?' asked Jack, who was half-asleep himself.

"Just jot down what you think we should do"

[PLAIN OR RINGLETS]

"'Oh, that Mister Something !—he'll be the death of me !' observed his lordship.

"'I thought so,' replied Jack ; 'what's the chap been after now ?'

"'I dreamt he'd killed old Lablache—best hound I have,' replied his lordship.

"'He be ——,' grunted Jack.

"'Ah, it's all very well for you to say, "he be this" and "he be that," but I can tell you what, that fellow is going to be a very awkward customer—a terrible thorn in my side.'

"'Humph !' grunted Jack, who didn't see how.

"'There's mischief about that fellow,' continued his lordship, pouring himself out half a tumbler of gin, and filling it up with water. 'There's mischief about the fellow. I don't like his looks—I don't like his coat—I don't like his boots—I don't like anything about him. I'd rather see the back of him than the front. He must be got rid of,' added his lordship.

"'Well, I did my best to-day, I'm sure,' replied Jack. 'I was deuced near wanting the patent coffin you were so good as to promise me.'

"'You did your work *well*,' replied his lordship, 'you did your work well ; and you shall have my other specs till I can get you a new pair from town ; and if you'll serve me again, I'll remember you in my will—I'll leave you something handsome.'

"'I'm your man," replied Jack."

And in *Plain or Ringlets* Admiration Jack and Mr. Ballivant, the family lawyer, are discussing the question of marriage settlements.

"'Then how about the other property ?' asked Mr. Bunting, after a short pause.

"'The other property is very purty,' replied Mr. Ballivant, 'very purty for a single man's property, but it would hardly support the requirements of married life—not at least according to the high standard at which expectations are now pitched.'

"'Not if there's love on both sides ?' demanded Mr. Bunting eagerly.

"'I think not,' said Mr. Ballivant drily, with an ominous shake of his head.

Mr. Bunting gasped for breath.

"'The fact is,' said Ballivant *sotto voce*, 'we have two strings to our bow and can afford to be a little fastidious.'

"'I see,' said Mr. Bunting resignedly.

"'Not that I advocate mercenary matches,' observed Mr. Ballivant, 'but every day's experience shows one the necessity of prudence and caution.'

"'No doubt,' replied Mr. Bunting, 'no doubt—only when there is mutual attachment and tolerable sufficiency it seems hard.'

"'True,' rejoined Mr. Ballivant, 'true, only sufficiency is a thing that no one has ever been able to define. It is something like riches—a man considers himself rich enough when he has got a little more than he has. People want to begin life where their parents used to end it. Women are educated now solely for the ornamental.'

"'Well, but am I to understand that all this comes from the young lady herself?' asked Mr. Bunting.

"'To a certain extent—to a certain extent,' replied Mr. Ballivant."

The man who can write those pieces of dialogue—those and hundreds as good—is plainly a master of his craft. There is nothing forced or unnatural about them, they are simply the talk of ordinary people written down as if it had just been overheard. It is perfectly in character with the speakers and with their mood at the moment: Lord Scamperdale depressed and apprehensive, Jack Spraggon sleepy and indifferent; Mr. Ballivant pedantic and discouraging, Admiration Jack propitiatory and crestfallen. Surtees must have had as keen an ear for speech as an eye for appearance. His dialogue is always—as the speech of ordinary men is always—disjointed, ungrammatical, allusive and above all repetitive. Indeed one of the commonest habits of people in ordinary talk is repeating themselves, and repeating, too, the last words of the previous speaker. How well Surtees had appreciated this habit is shown in the dialogue quoted above, in Lord Scamperdale's "There's mischief about that fellow. There's mischief about that fellow" and "You did your work well. You did your work well," in Mr. Ballivant's "No doubt, no doubt" and "True, true" and "To a certain extent—to a certain extent."

The most repetitive person—because he is the most boring conversationalist—in all the books is Sir Moses Mainchance.

"'Ay, come in!' cried Cuddy, leading the way; 'come in, and get Mr. Pringle a drop of brandy, for he's eaten something that's disagreed with him.'

"Eaten something that's disagreed with him. Sorry to hear that; what could it be?—what could it be?" asked Sir Moses, as the party now groped their way along the back passages.

"'Why, I blame the partridge pie,' replied Cuddy demurely.

"'Not a bit of it!' rejoined Sir Moses—'not a bit of it! Ate some myself—ate some myself—will finish it now—will finish it now.'

"'We've saved you that trouble,' replied Cuddy, 'for we finished it ourselves.'

"'The deuce you did!' exclaimed Sir Moses, adding, 'and were *you* sick?'

"'Squeamish,' replied Cuddy—'Squeamish; not so bad as Mr. Pringle.'

"'But bad enough to want some brandy, I suppose,' observed the Baronet, now entering the library.

"'Quite so,' said Cuddy—'quite.'

"'Why didn't you get some?—why didn't you get some?' asked the Baronet, moving towards the bell.

"'Because Bankhead has none out,' replied Mr. Cuddy, before Sir Moses rang.

"'None out!' retorted Sir Moses—'none out!—what! have you finished that too?'

"'Somebody has it seems,' replied Cuddy, quite innocently.

"'Well, then, I'll tell you what you must do—I'll tell you what you must do,' continued the Baronet . . . 'you must go into the cellar yourself and get some—go into the cellar yourself and get some.'"

Whatever Surtees' faults as a stylist may have been he was never at a loss in reporting conversation. His accurate ear, his dislike of exaggeration and his keen sense of humour all helped him. They helped him to avoid the pitfalls that so many of his contemporaries fell into. His characters talk neither coherent prose nor over-forced comedy. They talk like the real people that they are.

VIII

For the Surtees' characters are real people. The same dislike of exaggeration which kept the dialogue within bounds and the same activity of eye and ear resulted in an endless succession of people in the novels who are as true and normal as those whom one meets in real life. It is often and with some truth observed of Dickens that his characters are caricatures, exaggerated and distorted to more than life-size. Perhaps it is for that reason that they appeal to most of us as Surtees' characters have never done. We can read about them, laugh and sympathize with them, without any uncomfortable feeling that we are laughing at or pitying ourselves. We can never, we feel, be as villainous as Quilp, as feckless as Micawber, as hypocritical as Pecksniff or as cruel as Squeers. There is something so exuberant and wholesale about the characters that they are lifted above the ordinary plane. Their worst vices become almost endearing—like the cruelty of Mr. Squeers when he remarked, "I never thrashed a boy in a hackney coach before—there's inconvenience in it, but the novelty gives it a certain relish," or like the humility of Uriah Heap when he believed he was "the 'umblest person living be the other who he may."

Surtees was a satirist, and it is the function of a satirist to make people uncomfortable. The nearer to their own level the satirist comes the more thoroughly he gets his effect. And Surtees' characters are very near our level. Thomas Seccombe dismissed them as coarse; Professor Saintsbury called them artificial-picaresque; and the Hon. J. W. Fortescue, following Seccombe, attributed the success of the characters more to Leech than to Surtees. "Without John Leech, an incomparably greater man, he would long ago have been forgotten." There is, one feels, beneath all these unfavourable opinions a sense of discomfort—the discomfort of seeing ourselves as a shrewd and merciless observer sees us.

But the final test and justification of a novelist's characters are whether they remain gratefully in the memory. They may represent qualities or states of mind, they may personify virtues and vices, but unless they have vitality and truth in themselves they can never endure. And it is because Surtees' characters are so vital and so true that they have survived to this day.

Surtees used, over and over again, the device of bringing together at the end of the book all the characters in it very much in the fashion of a pantomime. And imagination plays lovingly with the idea of one last great rally of all the characters in all the books.

It is tempting to place it in the familiar setting of the grand finale of a north-country pantomime—the stage crowded with huntsmen, whippers-in, grooms, butlers, maid-servants and ostlers; the gilded and brilliantly lit staircase at the back, down which come the characters two by two to make their final bow: Swig and Chowey, Mr. and Mrs. Barnington; Sir Moses and Lady Mainchance, Tom Scott and Septimus Muff—till, to the sound of hunting horns, Prince Charming and his Princess bring the procession to a close. But there imagination breaks down at the thought of a Princess with false ringlets and gooseberry eyes and of a Prince " rigged for 'unting but wearing 'is 'at instead of 'is cap," probably feeling as if he'd " eat a straw 'at or a pair o' worsted stockin's "—and almost certainly ejaculating audibly, " 'Oookey Valker."

For Surtees' world—like Chaucer's and unlike Dickens's—is a " field full of folk," and it is only in the hunting field that we can properly take leave of Mr. Jorrocks and his company—at some Grand Union Hunt after a celestial fox through the Elysian Fields. The pack is Mr. Romford's, since, however he acquired them, they are the best hounds in any of the books and Facey himself rides close behind them with Frostyface and James Pigg beside him. On their heels come the top-sawyers, " the buoys who know how to go " ; Soapey Sponge and Lucy Glitters, Lord Scamperdale and that " fine natural blackguard " Jack Spraggon, Jovey Jessop and his Jug ; Pomponius Ego with both eyes on the hounds, Lord Ladythorne with one eye on hounds and the other on Miss de Glancy ; and, straggling behind, the ruck of the field : Tom Hall, Billy Bunting, Admiration Jack, Cuddy Flintoff, Caingey Thornton and the rest, while Colonel Blunt and the Heavysteed Dragoons and Billy Bobbinson and his Yeomanry bring up the rear.

The hunt sweeps by, leaving a trail of black hoof-marks on the spongy grass. But surely something or somebody is missing. And, as we strain our eyes and ears to catch the last sight and sound of the receding hunt there comes another sound behind us—laboured breathing, the slapping of great hooves, the crack of a crop on lean ribs. A gaunt brown horse with a roman nose and a rat-tail comes to a slithering stop and a voice, husky with exertion (and brandy and water), demands, " Pray my good man, 'ave you see my 'ounds ? Mr. Jorrocks's 'ounds in fact." But before the question is answered the horn sounds faint and clear, and far away and on a breath of wind there is carried back the cry of hounds. The rat-tail quivers, the roman nose twitches and the husky voice ejaculates, " Come hup ! you hugly brute ! Come hup I say ! " Arterxerxes breaks into a canter and the immortal voice grows fainter till we can barely catch the words, " rayther 'ave a field of corn than the finest run wot ever was seen." There is a convenient gap in the next fence, and as the sound of horn and cry of hounds come once again they are up and over. The rat-tail and the pink coat vanish from sight and the pounding hooves die away into the distance.

BIBLIOGRAPHY

Robert Smith Surtees. FREDERICK WATSON, 1933

Robert Smith Surtees, Creator of 'Jorrocks,' 1803-1864, by himself and E. D. CUMING, Edinburgh, 1924.

History of Hunting. PATRICK CHALMERS

Records of the Chase. " CECIL "

Northern Tours. " NIMROD "

Life of John Mitton. " NIMROD "

Reminiscences of the late T. Assheton Smith. SIR J. E. EARDLEY WILMOT, BART.

Thoughts on Hunting. PETER BECKFORD

The Character of England. Edited by ERNEST BARKER

Life of John Leech. W. P. FRITH, R.A.

W. Harrison Ainsworth and His Friends. S. M. ELLIS

Thackeray. MALCOLM ELWIN

English Coloured Books. MARTIN HARDIE

English Book Illustration. PHILIP JAMES

The English Novel. Prof. GEORGE SAINTSBURY

Nineteenth-Century Literature. Prof. GEORGE SAINTSBURY

Articles in *Blackwood's Magazine* by Miss Moira O'Neill and in *The Times Literary Supplement* by Professor B. Dobrée.

Novels by " Nimrod," Whyte-Melville, Charles and Henry Kingsley, F. E. Smedley, John Mills, A. Smith, and other nineteenth-century sporting novelists.

INDEX